LIVING FREE IN
ENEMY
TERRITORY

LIVING FREE IN ENEMY TERRITORY

CHRIST'S TRIUMPH OVER SATAN

GREG DUTCHER

DISCOVERY HOUSE
PUBLISHERS®

Discovery House Publishers is affiliated with RBC Ministries,
Grand Rapids, Michigan.

Requests for permission to quote from this book should be directed to:
Permissions Department, Discovery House Publishers, P.O. Box 3566,
Grand Rapids, MI 49501, or contact us by e-mail at
permissionsdept@dhp.org

Interior design by Sherri L. Hoffman

Printed in the United States of America

Third printing in 2012

To Steve Leslie
It is an honor to have a father-in-law who unashamedly loves Jesus.
Yet it is a greater honor when that man is a trusted friend,
one who sticks closer than a brother. I've got your back, Steve,
just as you've always had mine.

Be my comforter, light, guide, sanctifier;
Take of the things of Christ and show them to my soul;
Through thee may I daily learn more of his love,
     grace, compassion, faithfulness, beauty;
Lead me to the cross and show me his wounds,
     the hateful nature of evil, the power of Satan;
May I there see my sins as
     the nails that transfixed him,
     the cords that bound him,
     the thorns that tore him,
     the sword that pierced him.
Help me to find in his death the reality
     and immensity of his love.

—*The Valley of Vision*

Jesus, I am blind—be my light;
Darkened in my mind—be my wisdom;
Bend my stubborn will to Your own,
Open up my ears to hear Your Spirit.
Melt my conscience once again,
Help me hate the slightest sin,
And when Satan comes to tempt me . . .

I come running to You
When I fear, when I'm tried;
I come running to You
To Your blood, to Your side.
And there my soul finds rest,
There my soul finds rest—in You
My soul finds rest in You.

—Mark Altrogge, based on the prayer
"Need of Jesus" from *The Valley of Vision*

CONTENTS

FOREWORD

As far back as six centuries before Christ, soldiers have been taught a simple strategy: know your enemy. It was the famed Chinese general and strategist Sun Tzu who coined the phrase, and it reveals an important truth. If forced to do battle, an army gains a distinct advantage by knowing everything about who it battles.

The call to follow Christ is a call to war. Every Christian wages a lifelong, all-out war against the world, the flesh, and the Devil. Satan was man's first adversary, and he will be his adversary to the end. Yes, Satan's reign was broken at the cross, but for the time being he still wields his power as we await Christ's return.

It is good to know your enemy. Yet there is a particular temptation that comes with knowing your enemy: you may inadvertently become like him. They say that the way to train people to identify counterfeit currency is not to have them study counterfeit money but to study the real thing. When we know what is true, what is genuine, we are equipped to quickly recognize and root out what is false.

In *Living Free in Enemy Territory*, a book that deals specifically with Satan, Greg Dutcher takes just that kind of approach. Instead of dwelling on the person and work of Satan, he dwells upon Scripture, upon God's source of light and truth. And in the light of Scripture, Satan looks exceedingly dark and his work outrageously horrifying.

As much as it is good to know your enemy, it is even better to know the One who can smash—who has smashed!—the head of that enemy. Dutcher does an admirable job of drawing the reader to the work of Christ, to the One who has done just that. This short book shows how to live free in enemy territory. And the way to do that is not to ignore the Enemy, but neither is it to dwell upon him. The way to live free is to bow before the One who has already conquered Satan and who now waits for the day when He will destroy him forever.

Tim Challies
Author of *The Discipline of Spiritual Discernment*
www.challies.com

PART ONE

SEEING SATAN THROUGH HOLLYWOOD'S HAZE

There are two equal and opposite errors into which our race can fall about the devils. One is to disbelieve in their existence. The other is to believe, and to feel an excessive and unhealthy interest in them. They themselves are equally pleased by both errors and hail a materialist or a magician with the same delight.

—C. S. LEWIS, *THE SCREWTAPE LETTERS*

Jesus again said to them . . . "The thief comes only to steal and kill and destroy. I came that they may have life and have it abundantly."

—JOHN 10:10

CHAPTER ONE

THE PROBLEM WITH PITCHFORKS AND RED SATIN JUMPSUITS

Take a trip with me back to the summer of 1985. "We Are the World" was heard about sixty times a day on the radio. New Coke, after a dismal three-month debut, was about to be shelved for good to make room for Coca-Cola Classic. And Marty McFly desperately needed 1.21 gigawatts to power his DeLorean's flux capacitor to get "back to the future." It was also the year that I started wondering about Satan.

That summer my parents got cable television, and my brother and I began sneaking downstairs every night to experience the adolescent thrill of being scared to death. Every night a deranged serial killer, an evil spirit with a creepy name like "incubus" or "poltergeist," or an eerily humanlike robot from some other time or dimension was rampaging through modern suburbia. Andy and I would mock the movies as they unfolded their gory narratives on our living room Zenith. We were cool—just watching this stuff for fun. Well, maybe my brother was; I was transfixed by the terror. The Freddies and Jasons were tolerable; the robots and aliens were laughable; but the spirits and supernatural villains made me . . . uncomfortable.

During that same season, my good friend Matt was sharing the radical news of the gospel with me, and in the summer of 1985

I was still resisting the message. The thought that a good kid who usually listened to his parents (except for sneaking downstairs to watch horror flicks) could die and go to hell for not believing in Jesus seemed ridiculous to me. But God was working on my heart.

It would be over a year from that summer before I surrendered my life in faith to Christ, but God was preparing me. And my infatuation with evil spirits, demons, and incubuses (or was it incubi?) was to become one more link in the chain leading to my conversion. Late at night, after I checked under the bed and deep in the closet, I would lay in bed asking a lot of questions. *Is there a devil? If he's a spirit, how can anyone be safe from him? What if he targeted me? What could he do? Could I stop him? How could I stop him? What if I can't stop him?*

A lot has changed in my life since that summer. I have now been captivated with Jesus Christ as my first love, my heart's greatest treasure, for twenty-five years. And I have been a pastor for fourteen years—not quite a veteran, but seasoned enough to know a thing or two about the "spirit realm." Yet I want to start this book wearing a different hat (eventually, I'll put my pastor's cap on, I'm sure): a father's hat.

My wonderful wife, Lisa, and I have four great kids: two girls and two boys. Our second child, Benjamin, is a sensitive soul. He cares about animals, friends, even his siblings! He feels things deeply, and sometimes that comes out in his dreams. One of the greatest privileges I have is to be his snuggler when he climbs in between his mother and me after a bad dream. Some of his dreams are typical—hungry sharks, roaring lions, even being lost in a busy crowd. But a few of them are . . . well, strange.

Occasionally Ben tells me about a shadow, a voice, or a dark figure. In no way am I suggesting that all of these dreams are manifestations of satanic power; but I'm not prepared to say the opposite either. The realm of angels and demons is a mysterious territory for us humans (even though many televangelists seem to disagree). So rather than recalling each one of my son's nightmares, seeking to analyze whether there was actually a demon lurking in the shadows, I'd rather ask a more important question: What do I tell my son when he's clinging to me under the blankets in the wee hours of the morning?

> The realm of angels and demons is a mysterious territory for us humans.

Should I pull him close to my chest and say, "Benjamin—yes—Satan may be hiding under your bed, but just make sure to say your prayers"?

Or how about, "Now listen, Ben. Satan is a monster who wants to hurt you, but be a good soldier, go back to bed, and remember the verse I talked about"?

And if he's still scared, maybe I should suggest that we go into his room and together we will cast out the demons as a father and son activity, sort of like a three-legged race, but this time it is our determination to wipe out the guy in the red satin jumpsuit that ties us together.

THE HAZE OF HOLLYWOOD

All of these responses assume something—that Satan is a monster, not much different than the Freddies and Jasons that my brother and I grew up watching on our living room television.

One of the reasons I am writing this book is my concern that pop culture has shaped our view of Satan more than the Bible has. Hollywood has won the PR war in representing Satan. They've made him the ultimate horror movie villain, an amalgamation of every mad scientist, serial killer, and monster we've ever seen on the big screen. Sadly, sometimes a "Christian" song or book struts on the scene with a very similar-looking Satan. And many Christians assume they are getting the Bible's straight talk on Satan (after all, it was purchased at a Christian bookstore!), when they are really just getting a Hollywood devil with a little "Christian" flavor drizzled on top.

Pop culture has shaped our view of Satan more than the Bible has.

As with any caricature, there is a strand of truth in this portrait, but a thin strand indeed. There are some frightening portrayals of Satan in Scripture, as we will consider in chapter 2. But even these differ radically from the "when is the killer going to jump out from behind the door" scenes so common in Hollywood's portrayal of Satan. Movies like *Rosemary's Baby, The Exorcist,* and *Paranormal Activity* have given us a Satan whose deep voice and red eyes make us cower in our seats or hide under the covers, but they bear no resemblance to the Bible's description of our ancient enemy. Perhaps this is why some find it so difficult to say that they believe in Satan when incredulous people ask about his existence. The folks asking have seen the same movies, and they just can't believe that we cannot discern the difference between Hollywood and real life.

But forget Hollywood. What does Jesus say about the Devil?

JESUS DOESN'T BLUSH WHEN HE TALKS ABOUT SATAN

Consider the following statements Jesus makes about the Devil:

> "When anyone hears the word of the kingdom and does not understand it, the evil one comes and snatches away what has been sown in his heart." (Matthew 13:19)

> "And if Satan casts out Satan, he is divided against himself. How then will his kingdom stand?" (Matthew 12:26)

And he said to them, "I saw Satan fall like lightning from heaven." (Luke 10:18)

The Savior speaks of Satan's reality in the same matter-of-fact way that He talks about faith, repentance, love, marriage, adultery, divorce, money, prayer, and fasting. Apparently Jesus did not think that acknowledging the very real presence of Satan would ruin His credibility. The Son of God knew who the Devil truly is, and He was not shy about calling him out. Perhaps the most striking example of this is found in John 10:10!

> **The Son of God knew who the Devil truly is, and He was not shy about calling him out.**

"The thief comes only to steal and kill and destroy. I came that they may have life and have it abundantly."

This is a remarkable passage. Not only does Jesus leave no doubt concerning the Devil's existence, but He actually uses Satan's character as a contrast to His own![1] Just as a jeweler lays a precious diamond on a piece of black velvet, so Jesus draws our attention to His glorious character by setting it against the dark backdrop of Satan's despicable nature.

---

1. Not all commentators agree that Jesus is referring to Satan in this passage. Some see merely a contrast between the idea of a thief and the idea of a shepherd. I subscribe to A. W. Pink's argument that "it will be observed that Christ here uses the singular number. In verse 8 He had spoken of 'thieves and robbers' when referring to all who had come before Him; but here in verse 10 He has some particular individual in view." But even those who don't think Jesus is necessarily describing Satan in this passage should be able to see this passage as applicable to the Devil's nature, since earlier in John's gospel Jesus describes him as "'a murderer from the beginning, and [who] has nothing to do with the truth, because there is no truth in him. When he lies, he speaks out of his own character, for he is a liar and the father of lies'" (John 8:44).

So if the Lord himself wants us to contemplate just who He is in contrast with Satan,[2] then I say, "Let's do it!"

LIVING FREE IN ENEMY TERRITORY—NOT JUST A TITLE

And so back to my original question: What do I tell my son about Satan? When my son snuggles with me under our comforter in the wee hours of the morning, I don't want to reinforce some silly picture that a Hollywood filmmaker has concocted to entice a thrill-seeking teenager. Nor do I want my son to be more preoccupied with Satan's glitz than with the Savior's grace. What I want is for my son to understand who Satan is in relation to Jesus so that he can drift back to sleep in peace, knowing that the Devil is a defeated foe.

And make no mistake—the Bible makes it crystal clear that Jesus has defeated our ancient enemy. Consider the following passages:

Make no mistake—the Bible makes it crystal clear that Jesus has defeated our ancient enemy.

And immediately there was in their synagogue a man with an unclean spirit. And he cried out, "What have you to do with us, Jesus of Nazareth? Have you come to destroy us? I know who you are—the Holy One of God." (Mark 1:23–24)

"Now is the judgment of this world; now will the ruler of this world be cast out." (John 12:31)

The reason the Son of God appeared was to destroy the works of the devil. (1 John 3:8)

---

2. In chapter 11 we will revel in this kind of contemplation. By contrasting the King of Glory with the Father of Lies, my hope is that you will experience a renewed love and allegiance for Jesus as your greatest treasure.

But we will never appreciate the Satan-crushing work of Jesus if we do not understand who Satan really is. If he is some gruesome serial killer or special-effects monster, then Jesus' victory will look less glorious than it truly is. If Satan's chief role in the world is to make us scared of things that go bump in the night, then the transforming realities of the cross and the empty tomb will seem little better than a child's night-light that keeps the bogeyman away.

Do you want to understand the fullness of Jesus' victory over Satan? Do you want to experience the truth of the power that "he who is in you is greater than he who is in the world" (1 John 4:4)? If you do, and I pray that you do, the only way forward is to properly understand who Satan is and what Satan does.

In the final editing stages of my first book, *You Are the Treasure That I Seek*, my editor-turned-friend, Annette, sent me a gem to include in the appendix. A largely forgotten hymn, "Jesus, Priceless Treasure," was a wonderfully unexpected blessing to include in the closing pages of that work. And I would like to include it in the beginning pages of this one. Notice particularly the opening line of the third stanza.

> Jesus, priceless treasure,
> Source of purest pleasure,
> Truest friend to me.
> Long my heart was burning,
> And my soul was yearning,
> Lord, with you to be!
> Yours I am, O spotless Lamb;
> Nothing I'll allow to hide you,
> Nothing ask beside you.
>
> In your arms I rest me;
> Foes who would molest me

Cannot reach me here.
Though the earth be shaking,
Every heart be quaking,
Jesus calms my fear.
Sin and hell in conflict fell
With their bitter storms assail me;
Jesus will not fail me.

Satan, I defy you;
Death, I now decry you;
Fear, I bid you cease.
World, you cannot harm me
Nor your threats alarm me
While I sing of peace.
God's great power guards every hour;
Earth and all its depths adore Him,
Silent bow before Him.

Hence, all earthly treasure!
Jesus is my pleasure,
Jesus is my choice.
Hence, all empty glory!
What to me your story
Told with tempting voice?
Pain or loss or shame or cross
Shall not from my Savior move me
Since He chose to love me.

Hence, all fears and sadness,
For the Lord of gladness,
Jesus, enters in.
Those who love the Father,
Though the storms may gather,

Still have peace within.
For, whatever I must bear,
Still in you lies purest pleasure,
Jesus, priceless treasure!
                                        —Johann Franck

In many ways, the book before you is an unfolding of this entire hymn. My prayer for you is that you would know the joy of what it means to be liberated by Jesus Christ, our priceless treasure, and to be set free from the enemy of your soul.

The journey will not be easy, however. We must start by doing the work of a profiler to discover: Who is Satan? What is his chief aim in the world and in our lives?

I won't lie to you; the answers to these questions are troubling. But by understanding the power and purpose of our great adversary, the superior power and purpose of Jesus Christ will emerge.

QUESTIONS FOR REFLECTION

1. Do you have a memory of how you pictured the Devil when you were younger? Was he scary? Goofy? Irrelevant? Did you view him as a real threat?

2. Are you embarrassed to talk about Satan as a real being in the presence of a skeptic? Why?

3. Read Matthew 12:26, 13:19, and Luke 10:18. Obviously, Jesus had no hesitation in talking about Satan. Based on these three passages alone (don't import or include what you already know), describe a preliminary sketch of the Devil as Jesus sees him.

4. Read John 10:10. In light of the comparison between Jesus and the thief, do you agree with the author that we will not fully appreciate Jesus and His work if we don't take a long, hard look at Satan? Why or why not?

Myths which are believed in tend to become true.

—GEORGE ORWELL

The great enemy of truth is very often not the lie—deliberate, contrived, and dishonest—but the myth—persistent, persuasive, and unrealistic. Too often we hold fast to the clichés of our forebears. We subject all facts to a prefabricated set of interpretations. We enjoy the comfort of opinion without the discomfort of thought.

—JOHN F. KENNEDY

See to it that no one takes you captive by philosophy and empty deceit, according to human tradition, according to the elemental spirits of the world, and not according to Christ.

—COLOSSIANS 2:8

CHAPTER TWO

DISPELLING TWO MYTHS ABOUT SATAN

Myths are powerful. They can change the way people live, and sometimes the way people die. For centuries a myth that the earth was flat kept sailors from venturing out too far in uncertain waters lest they fall off the edge of the world. In ancient Egypt a myth prompted loved ones to bury their dead with beer and bread since such sustenance would be needed in the long journey of the afterlife. Today countless Elvis devotees flock to gas stations on deserted highways across America because someone swears they saw the King of Rock 'n' Roll getting his pink Cadillac filled up in the full service lane. (Someone needs to tell these misguided folks, "Hey, that's just a myth, thank you, thank you very much.") Myths are simply mistaken beliefs. But beliefs matter!

As a pastor I have had many sincere Christians share their concerns about Satan and his activities with me.

"I'm wondering if my teenager may be plagued by a demon?"

"We got rid of our daughter's dolls when we found out they were made in Haiti. We thought they might have been cursed by a voodoo practitioner."

"Pastor, we were wondering if you could come over and pray over each room to make sure that there is no satanic presence there."

The concerns these people have are very real to them, and I do not mean to mock their fears. However, much of this speculation about demons and demonic activity seems to be informed by movies and television rather than the Bible. I also wonder how many of these concerns are rooted in Hollywood's portrayal of the Devil instead of Scripture—because it seems that two key myths have slipped into the thinking of many Christians.

> Much of this speculation about demons and demonic activity seems to be informed by movies and television rather than the Bible.

MYTH #1: SATAN AS A SCALY BEAST

As we discussed in chapter 1, Hollywood has successfully created a Satan who scares us to death. But why are we so frightened of this special-effects creature, with its scaly body, red glowing eyes, and sharp horns? If we are honest it's probably because an entity who can make the lights go out, drop the room temperature to arctic levels, and talk in a deep and creepy voice has a lot of power to raise the goose bumps on our flesh. The ending of the movie *Rosemary's Baby* was unnerving because we feared that we would steal a glimpse of the baby—the child of Satan. As the cultic followers on the screen were fawning over the demon child, those in the audience were on the edge of their seats, wanting to see but afraid to look.

And therein lies our great problem: we are obsessed with Satan's physicality. What does he look like? Where does he set up shop? What will I do if he holes up in my daughter's doll collection? Such questions spark great ideas for horror writers, filmmakers, and special effects experts, but they don't help us think biblically about Satan and his minions.

As we will discover in the next chapter, we will only be able to spot our enemy's presence and activity if we know his true identity.

Yet if we keep living under the delusion that he is the Creature from the Black Lagoon, then we will inevitably fall prey to the second myth.

MYTH #2: SATAN AS AN ALL-POWERFUL, OMNIPRESENT FORCE

The fifteen-year-old, cable-movie-addicted version of myself was distraught over something that seemed fundamentally unfair. It seemed that Satan and his demons were not only powerful, but free to move about wherever and whenever they wanted. In movie after movie, a normal American family moved into the one house that the Devil had arbitrarily chosen as his summer vacation home. And once he did, no amount of holy water or exorcisms could stop him from destroying the house, the people living in it (including the faithful family dog), and anyone or anything that tried to stand in his way. If Satan wanted to paint a bull's-eye on your back, then too bad for you! Sometimes popular Christian teaching presents a Satan with this kind of unstoppable power and authority. The repercussions of such a portrayal are troubling, as we will see.

When I started to wonder about a possible spiritual realm and this free reign of Satan, I sometimes scared myself into virtual paralysis. A pimple-faced teenager had no recourse if satanic forces made him a target. Yet I believe that many Christians, even mature Christians, think about Satan in the same way.

I recently asked a group of twenty-somethings two questions:

1) Can Satan go wherever he wants to?
2) Can Satan make your life a living hell if wants to?

Ask yourself these same two questions. If you answered yes to either of them (as the twenty-somethings did to both), then I have news for you. The bad news is that you've been duped into believing the myth that Satan is an all-powerful, omnipresent force. The good news is that you can get *unduped*!

SATAN IS NOT BEASTLY, BUT BEAUTIFUL

While the Bible is sparse on any physical description of Satan, it gives us enough clues that we can be certain he is not some hideous creature who would make our skin crawl. When the apostle Paul warned the church at Corinth about the Devil's activity, he urged them to be on the lookout for beauty, not beastliness.

> For such men are false apostles, deceitful workmen, disguising themselves as apostles of Christ. And no wonder, for *even Satan disguises himself as an angel of light*. (2 Corinthians 11:13–14)

God's enemy often uses false teachers to do his bidding. But the false teacher is not some ugly, deformed ogre who stands in a pulpit and urges his listeners to tear up their Bibles in their pews. On the contrary, he can be a well-dressed, smiling preacher, with perfectly white capped teeth, who looks like he sincerely wants to be your advocate. And who is this false teacher modeling? Satan himself—who presents himself as an angel of light.

Some commentators use this passage to suggest that Satan is really hideous in his appearance, but Paul does not seem to be suggesting that here. He is contrasting the outward appearance of false teachers with their inward motivations: outwardly they are pleasant, but inwardly their motives are sinister. Paul is not suggesting that Satan is actually physically ugly behind his façade. He is merely demonstrating that Satan has sinister motives, but that his outward manifestations can be quite beautiful. Satan's physical appearance is never really the issue, because Satan is an angel—an incorporeal being. That should not surprise us in light of the Devil's origin.

Bible commentators also debate certain Old Testament passages that may or may not chronicle Satan's fall from heaven.[1] The two main passages are Isaiah 14:12–15 and Ezekiel 28:15–17. Both passages describe the mighty fall of a glorious ruler whose pride swelled to the point of rebellion. As appealing as it is to link these passages to Satan's downfall, the problem is that Isaiah refers to the king of Babylon and Ezekiel refers to the king of Tyre. Based on certain New Testament passages, however, it is reasonable to conclude that there was some sort of angelic rebellion in ages past and that Satan was once an angel who rebelled against God and was expelled from His presence.

> When the apostle Paul warned the church at Corinth about the Devil's activity, he urged them to be on the lookout for beauty not beastliness.

> If God did not spare the angels who sinned, but cast them down to hell and delivered them into chains of darkness, to be reserved for judgment. (2 Peter 2:4 NKJV)

> And the angels who did not keep their proper domain, but left their own abode, He has reserved in everlasting chains under darkness for the judgment of the great day. (Jude 1:6 NKJV)

These passages paint a picture of a heavenly mutiny. A number of angels banded together in opposition against God, and God responded by banning them from heaven and marking them for eternal judgment. Yet neither of these passages mentions Satan.

---

1. For more detail see Wayne Grudem, *Systematic Theology,* chapter 20, "Satan and Demons" (Grand Rapids: Zondervan, 1994).

So how do we know he should be counted in their number? Jesus answers this question by giving us a glimpse of the original blueprint for hell, particularly for whom it was constructed.

> Then he will say to those on his left, "Depart from me, you cursed, into the eternal fire prepared for the devil and his angels." (Matthew 25:41)

Notice that phrase "the devil and his angels." The relationship is that of a leader and his followers, a president and his cabinet, a general and his soldiers. Satan is the ringleader of a band of angelic malcontents. So his essence is angelic, not bestial.

Satan is the ringleader of a band of angelic malcontents.

Now even as we say that, we don't want to make the mistake of assuming that these angels are the cute and cuddly Hallmark variety. Every time angels show up in Scripture, they have to say, "Don't be afraid!"[2] Angels are an awesome sight—*but* they are not monsters. So Satan is not a monster either.

SATAN IS NOT ALL-POWERFUL

As much as Satan would love to be free to do whatever he pleases, to roam at will throughout the earth, the world is not his playground—at least not in the way he wants it to be. While Satan may have carte blanche freedom in screenplays and novels, God gives him no such liberty in the real world.

The perfect example of the extent of Satan's "freedom" is found in the book of Job. There we learn that Satan desires to test Job, a righteous servant of God (Job 1). That's all a modern filmmaker would need to make a horror flick. From that point Satan would

---

2. Even in the joyful narrative of Luke's Christmas story, the awesome spectacle that angels present cannot be missed. See Luke 1:11–13, 1:30, 2:9–10.

plot his evil plans to ruin Job and his family in full computer-generated special effects glory. But the Bible has a scene that would ruin the producer's vision.

> And the LORD said to Satan, "Behold, all that [Job] has is in your hand. Only against him do not stretch out your hand." So Satan went out from the presence of the LORD. (Job 1:12)

What? God puts limits on Satan's plans? He is not free to move about the world as he pleases? That's right! Satan is not only limited by God in what he can and cannot do, but Satan must also *ask* God's permission before he can do anything! In the New Testament, Jesus confirms this limit on Satan's freedom in a stern warning to the apostle Peter. Shortly before Jesus' death, He wants to prepare Peter for a coming test.

> "Simon, Simon, behold, Satan demanded to have you, that he might sift you like wheat, but I have prayed for you that your faith may not fail." (Luke 22:31–32)

Satan is not only limited by God in what he can and cannot do, but Satan must also *ask* God's permission before he can do anything!

Notice that Satan "demanded" to have Peter. He *demanded*. But demand is not the same as *command*. People can demand all they want. A prisoner without the possibility of parole can demand that he be released, but he has no control over his destiny—that belongs to the parole board. The toddler can demand ice cream, but only his mother is tall enough to pull it from the freezer. It is no different with Satan. Yes, he demands, but it is God who determines whether his request will be granted. This is why Martin Luther is alleged to have said, "The devil is God's devil."

Make no mistake: Satan is evil. He is powerful. He seeks to do us great harm. But he is definitely not free!

WHO IS THE BIBLE'S "SMOKING MAN"?

In the TV series *The X-Files* there is an enigmatic character known as The Smoking Man. This character began appearing at the beginning of the series, and whenever he appeared he was smoking a cigarette. For years, one of the mysteries of *The X-Files* was the true identity of this character. Finally it was revealed that his name was C. G. B. Spender. But his name didn't tell us much. It wasn't until we learned he was working for a secret organization called The Syndicate, which was conspiring to cover up evidence of an alien race intent on colonizing the earth, that we really began to know who The Smoking Man was.

So it is with Satan. It is helpful to know a few facts about him. We know he is a rebellious and cast-out angel with a chip on his shoulder. We know he disguises himself as an angel of light. But what is his true identity? We will only know that by learning about his mission. Just what is he seeking to do? What is his end game?

Let's turn to these and other questions as the haze of Hollywood and the myths continue to evaporate.

QUESTIONS FOR REFLECTION

1. Can you think of a myth that you believed as a child—or maybe even as an adult? How did discovering the truth affect you?
2. Why do you think that "Satan as a Scaly Beast" is such a popular myth? Is there some justification for this portrait in the Bible?
3. Read 2 Corinthians 11:13–14. Why was it so important for the ancient church to understand what Paul was saying here? What

potential dangers would threaten them if they did not properly understand how Satan presents himself?

4.   Read Job 1:12 and Luke 22:31–32. How do the limits on Satan's freedom encourage you in your faith?

He saw a Lawyer killing a Viper
On a dung-hill beside his stable,
And the Devil smiled, for it put him in mind
Of Cain and his brother, Abel.

> —SAMUEL TAYLOR COLERIDGE,
> "THE DEVIL'S THOUGHTS"

"There's lotsa people here that hate me, lots. I can feel it. It's like bees stingin' me."

> —JOHN COFFEY, *THE GREEN MILE*

The accuser of our brethren.

> —REVELATION 12:10 NKJV

CHAPTER THREE

THE GLEEFUL PROSECUTOR

So if Satan isn't the bogeyman under the bed, or the psychopathic doll bent on destruction, or any other malevolent force fresh out of a Stephen King novel, then just who is he?

We might be tempted to think that classic literature gives us a better portrait, right? After all, doesn't the very adjective "classic" suggest a refined, balanced understanding and appreciation of life's realities? Yet we soon find that the classics have not helped us much either with gaining an accurate understanding of the Devil's nature. Neither Dante's half-frozen, three-headed beast in the center of hell, nor Milton's Tartarus-ruling dictator give us the Bible's crystal-clear profile of the Enemy of our souls.[1] A corrupt angel on a leash is only a partial identity. If he's after us, where, how, and to what end is he plotting? The answer to these questions is critical.

Imagine you are in a crowded mall and a police officer calls you on your cell phone. "We've just gotten word that someone's

---

1. These are references to Dante Alighieri, *The Comedy of Dante Alighieri: Cantica I: Hell,* trans. Dorothy L. Sayers (New York: Penguin Books, 1949), John Milton, *Paradise Lost* (New York: Penguin Classics, 2003). It should be noted that of the two literary giants, Milton's portrait of Satan is much closer to the Bible's. Milton emphasizes the Devil's cunning and remarkable ability to ensnare others with his wicked logic. Nevertheless, his infamous quote, "Better to reign in Hell, than to serve in Heaven," sadly reinforces the faulty idea that Satan is ruling over hell, something the Bible flatly denies.

taken out a contract on your life," he tells you. "There is a hit man in the food court watching you right now." Suddenly you are totally focused on the identity of that hit man. *Is he tall? Short? Bald? White? Black? Asian? Bearded? Fat? Thin? Is he on the other side of the court, or is he standing right next to me? Has he spotted me yet? Will he try to kill me here in the mall? Or will he lure me into a more secluded place?*

When a person means to do you harm, understanding that person's identity, appearance, whereabouts, modus operandi, intentions, and skills are things you must know.

The apostle Paul wanted the Christians at Corinth to be on guard so that they "would not be outwitted by Satan, for [they] are not ignorant of his designs" (2 Corinthians 2:11). He also warned the Ephesians that no matter how many opposed their stance for Christ, their real enemies were not people but the sinister forces lurking behind them; they were not wrestling "against flesh and blood, but against . . . the spiritual forces of evil in the heavenly places" (Ephesians 6:12). And Peter urged those under his care to be on the lookout for Satan, who "prowls around like a roaring lion, seeking someone to devour" (1 Peter 5:8).

Putting these three passages together, we can draw a preliminary sketch of our ancient enemy. He is a powerful spiritual being who is scheming to outwit us, and he is planning to pounce on us and eat us for breakfast! In light of this we should do our best to know just who this enemy is, don't you think?

A HELPFUL CLUE FROM THE BOOK OF JOB

It may seem counterintuitive *not* to start at Genesis in our quest to understand the identity of Satan. However, the Serpent's abrupt presence in the garden of Eden can be better understood once we learn a little more about Satan's modus operandi. To do that, we return to the book of Job, where we are given an unusual opportunity to eavesdrop on a conversation between God and the Devil.

> Now there was a day when the sons of God came to present themselves before the Lord, and Satan also came among them. The LORD said to Satan, "From where have you come?"
>
> Satan answered the LORD and said, "From going to and fro on the earth, and from walking up and down on it."
>
> And the LORD said to Satan, "Have you considered my servant Job, that there is none like him on the earth, a blameless and upright man, who fears God and turns away from evil?"
>
> Then Satan answered the LORD and said, "Does Job fear God for no reason? Have you not put a hedge around him and his house and all that he has, on every side? You have blessed the work of his hands, and his possessions have increased in the land. But stretch out your hand and touch all that he has, and he will curse you to your face." (Job 1:6–11)

This passage is filled with intrigue. There is some debate among Bible commentators as to where this meeting is taking place and what exactly is going on. Some suggest that the "sons of God" are not angels, but Job's sons who are worshipping before the Lord, so that the passage is to be understood as Satan invisibly slipping himself into the scene, where only God can see him in the spiritual realm. But I think a greater argument can be made that the "sons of God" are, indeed, angels, and for sovereign purposes, God is allowing Satan to make an appearance in His heavenly court.

Since the God of the universe is going to have a conversation with the greatest villain in the universe, however, for our purposes here, we are more interested in what is said. The conversation centers on the legitimacy of Job's trust in God. Does Job love God for being

God or simply for the good stuff God gives? Satan is convinced that Job only "loves" God because God is Job's own personal genie in the sky. If Satan can only have his way with Job for a few minutes, then Job's righteous veneer will vanish.

Satan is pouring all of his energy into one grand outcome: the cursing of God. That's his end game.

Here is where we begin to see the clear light of Scripture dispel the myths that have been cast around the person of Satan. The popular culture version of Satan wants to physically hurt us; usually he wants to kill us. But the biblical Satan has a much more ambitious goal than doing us bodily harm. That's child's play for him. Satan is pouring all of his energy into one grand outcome: the cursing of God. That's his end game. He makes this clear in Job 1:11:

> But stretch out your hand and touch all that [Job] has, and he will curse you to your face.

Satan's main ambition can be clearly seen in the book of Job. The book starts with Job consistently praying that his children do not "curse God in their hearts." Then Satan enters the story with a goal to see Job himself curse God to His face. This background makes the words of Job's wife in chapter 2 particularly ominous: "Curse God and die." Job's wife has unknowingly become a mouthpiece for Satan himself.

If Satan can lure us into a place where we curse God, then he has won.

At this point it would be natural to ask what "cursing God" means, since most Christians would never think of actually shaking their fists in God's face and defying Him in such a dramatic manner. Yet "cursing God" appears to be one of many phrases that describe what Satan cherishes.

The apostle Paul summarizes Satan's aim as "[keeping us] from seeing the light of the gospel of the glory of Christ, who is the image of God" (2 Corinthians 4:4). In its context, this verse is describing Satan's work among unbelievers, but it is certainly a safe application to say that he does not want Christians to think glorious thoughts of Christ.

John Piper captures it well in *God Is the Gospel* when he writes, "Satan is not mainly interested in causing us misery. He is mainly interested in making Christ look bad. He hates Christ. And he hates the glory of Christ. He will do all he can to keep people from seeing Christ as glorious."

The devil loathes any thought of God's glory, Christ's glory, and the gospel's glory. If Job, or any believer, has diminished thoughts of God's glorious nature, then Satan has scored a significant victory. A well-dressed man politely telling his friend at Starbucks that the God of the Bible just doesn't seem like a God that's worthy of his worship is more of a victory for Satan than all the gore and terror in the world. If a husband starts to think that God is a bit old-fashioned in His hatred of adultery (after all, the secretary at his office understands him better than his wife does), then Satan has scored a victory. If a mother begins to think that traveling to exotic places is preferable to the daily grind of caring for small children, then the Devil has scored a victory.

> Satan is working with all of his might to block our view of God's awesome beauty and glory, His righteousness and justice.

Satan is working with all of his might to block our view of God's awesome beauty and glory, His righteousness and justice.

When he comes in roaring like a lion, it is to drown out our praise and adoration of God.

ADDING INSULT TO INJURY

It would be bad enough if Satan accomplished his vile mission of getting us to rob God of glory. But the Devil does not stop with inflicting that spiritual harm. His supreme delight appears to be in rubbing our faces in the very mess he has helped to create! In fact, now would be a good time to tell you that the word *devil* means "the accuser." When the Bible shines God's searchlight on Satan, we do not find him hiding in a closet or under the bed, excitedly waiting to terrify clueless suburbanites who don't have the common sense to leave the house. No, we find him in a much more respectable place—the courtroom.

A perfectly groomed man in a three-piece suit with a black leather briefcase takes his place before the judge's bench and calmly points at the defendant (yes, that's you and me). In his hand is a legal pad with line after line of our infractions against God's law neatly spelled out. And he skillfully makes his case. After all, he has been studying human behavior for millennia, and he has no trouble furnishing ample evidence of our guilt before God. If you think this scenario sounds too contrived, take a look at the vision the prophet Zechariah had of the high priest Joshua standing before the Lord.

> Then he showed me Joshua the high priest standing before the angel of the Lord, and Satan standing at his right hand to accuse him. (Zechariah 3:1)

Satan's ambitious goal was to discredit Joshua from standing in God's presence. It is interesting to note what drew the Devil's accusations in the first place: "Now Joshua was standing before the angel, clothed with filthy garments" (Zechariah 3:3). In ancient Israel, the high priest had the unique job of standing before God as the people's representative. If his "clothes" were dirty, then, by default, so were the people's clothes; and thus, everyone was doomed. The robes of the high priest were to be spotless, representing the kind of hearts his people were to have.[2] But like all mankind, Joshua is "filthy"—a true sinner. And who is right next to him? Satan—all dressed up for his closing argument.

This is Satan doing what he does best. In fact, when the book of Revelation celebrates his eventual downfall, our enemy is depicted in his role as a prosecuting attorney: "the accuser of our brothers has been thrown down, who accuses them day and night before our God" (Revelation 12:10).

The phrase "day and night" is used to describe people involved in their greatest passions and commitments. The Olympian trains day and night for the chance to win gold. The iPod-obsessed teenager listens to his tunes day and night, with no regard for nobler pursuits. The mother whose child has been abducted doesn't take a coffee break but waits and prays day and night for the return of her precious child.

> Satan's day and night passion is to accuse the very people he has tempted to sin in the first place!

Satan's day and night passion is to accuse the very people he has tempted to sin in the first place! Pouring salt in the wound he has ripped open, pressing down on the gash he has

---

2. It appears that one of the great aims of the book of the Leviticus is to leave the reader with a powerful sense of the need to be cleansed from impurity. Details about such things as clothes, sores, and washings remind us that "If any one of all your offspring throughout your generations approaches the holy things that the people of Israel dedicate to the LORD, while he has an uncleanness, that person shall be cut off from my presence: I am the LORD" (Leviticus 22:3).

inflicted, the Devil delights in adding insult to injury.[3] And oh, how those accusations sting!

In the movie *The Green Mile*, gentle giant John Coffey, who many think is intended to be a Christlike figure (notice the initials J. C.), describes the continual pain of living in a fallen world. "There's lotsa people here that hate me, lots. I can feel it. It's like bees stingin' me." This is a picture of what it feels like to be under Satan's continual accusations. He is a vile enemy, but we cannot deny the skill and passion he brings to his work.

SO, JUST WHO ARE WE UP AGAINST?

One of the movies that my brother and I watched late at night was *Terminator*, in which a futuristic, Schwarzenegger-looking robot is bent on accomplishing his mission to kill Sarah Connor, the mother of a yet-to-be-born child who will one day lead the resistance against the evil robots. But a young hero named Kyle Reese travels back in time to tell Sarah that she is in danger from this muscular killing machine. "Listen, and understand," he says of the villain. "That terminator is out there. It can't be bargained with. It can't be reasoned with. It doesn't feel pity, or remorse, or fear. And it absolutely will not stop, ever!"

Satan is out there. He can't be bargained with. He can't be reasoned with. He is pitiless and always laser-focused on his two-fold mission: 1) To lure us into a place where we turn against God, and then 2) To accuse us of our guilt for the very rebellion he's helped engineer. For the Christian, nothing could be more serious. If God is ignored, blamed, or rebelled against, then His glory will not be our joy. The world will not see us as "a chosen race, a royal

---

3. Chapter 8 will go into much more detail about the guilt that such accusation produces. More importantly, we will consider the antidote to the guilt that can so easily paralyze us.

priesthood, a holy nation, a people for his own possession, that you may proclaim the excellencies of him who called you out of darkness into his marvelous light (1 Peter 2:9)," but as a defeated, guilt-paralyzed, bunch of weird "religious" malcontents.

But how can any of us frail humans stand up against such an adversary? In the sobering words of writer R. Kent Hughes:

> I am no genius at mathematics, but even with my limited capabilities I could be terrific at math if I worked on it for 100 years (maybe!). If I labored at it for 1,000 years and read all the learned theories, I would be a Newton or an Einstein. Or what if I had 10,000 years? Given that time, any of us could become the world's greatest philosopher or psychologist or theologian or linguist . . . Satan has had multiple millennia to study and master the human disciplines, and when it comes to human subversion, he is the ultimate manipulator.

No mere human is a match for such an opponent. That realization can lead us to despair—or, it can lead us to the place it led Martin Luther when he penned his most famous hymn "A Mighty Fortress":

> For still our ancient foe
> Doth seek to work us woe;
> His craft and power are great,
> And armed with cruel hate,
> On earth is not his equal.
>
> Did we in our own strength confide,
> Our striving would be losing,
> Were not the right man on our side,
> The man of God's own choosing.

QUESTIONS FOR REFLECTION

1. In one sentence, do your best to define the aim of the Devil as it is presented by Hollywood.

2. Read Job 1:11. What is Satan's ultimate motive?

3. John Piper has written, "Satan is not mainly interested in causing us misery. He is mainly interested in making Christ look bad." Do you agree? Why do you think Satan hates Jesus so much?

4. Read 2 Corinthians 4:4. How should this passage affect your view of evangelism, particularly regarding the reasons people reject the gospel?

5. Read Zechariah 3:3. Can you think of a time when you felt "accused" the way Joshua is accused here?

PART TWO

SATAN'S D-DAY

It is the privilege of posterity to set matters right between those antagonists who, by their rivalry for greatness, divided a whole age.

—JOSEPH ADDISON

A lifetime of training for just ten seconds!

—JESSE OWENS

The reason the Son of God appeared was to destroy the works of the devil.

—1 JOHN 3:8

CHAPTER FOUR

SHOWDOWN—A PREVIEW OF THE COSMIC CLASH

Ali versus Frazier. Eliot Ness versus Al Capone. Batman versus the Joker. We love rivalries, don't we? But rivalries are just the necessary building blocks for what we really love. Showdowns!

Allow me to don my local sports hat and tell you that I am rarely more laser focused than when I watch my beloved Baltimore Ravens go up against the infamous Pittsburgh Steelers. And I'm not alone. Baltimore could be having its worse season ever, but just try to walk down to the Raven's stadium and purchase a ticket when the evil Black and Gold are in town (sorry Pittsburgh fans). It's always a sellout!

Every game in every sport is a competition, but only some games are showdowns. Every election is a competition, but only some are real showdowns. Yet you won't find a conflict in sports, politics, or any other realm that is as colossal as the showdown described in Matthew chapter 4.

Then Jesus was led up by the Spirit into the wilderness to be tempted by the devil. And after fasting forty days and forty nights, he was hungry. And the tempter came and said to him, "If you are the Son of God, command these stones to become loaves of bread." But he answered, "It is written,

"'Man shall not live by bread alone,
   but by every word that comes from the mouth
      of God.'"

Then the devil took him to the holy city and set him on the pinnacle of the temple and said to him, "If you are the Son of God, throw yourself down, for it is written,

"'He will command his angels concerning you,'

and

"'On their hands they will bear you up,
   lest you strike your foot against a stone.'"

Jesus said to him, "Again it is written, 'You shall not put the Lord your God to the test.'"

Again, the devil took him to a very high mountain and showed him all the kingdoms of the world and their glory. And he said to him, "All these I will give you, if you will fall down and worship me." Then Jesus said to him, "Be gone, Satan! For it is written,

"'You shall worship the Lord your God and him only shall you serve.'"

Then the devil left him, and behold, angels came and were ministering to him. (Matthew 4:1–11)

No competing sports teams, military generals, or world leaders could possibly match the magnitude of this rivalry. Here the mighty Son of God squares off with the cunning, crafty Serpent of old. One is determined to destroy us; the other has come to save us. Here, in the wilderness of Judea, the cosmic showdown takes place.

But have you ever asked this question: "Why was it necessary?"

BACK TO THE PREQUEL

Ever tried watching a sequel without watching the prequel? You miss a lot, don't you? The same is true here. To fully understand this encounter between Satan and the Savior, we must first go back to an eerily similar encounter that took place centuries before—the first showdown in the garden of Eden.

It is helpful to note at this point that in the New Testament Jesus is referred to as the "second Adam" or "last Adam" (1 Corinthians 15:45). So before we consider the heroic work of the second Adam, let's take a quick look at that first showdown in Paradise.

Now the serpent was more crafty than any other beast of the field that the LORD God had made.

He said to the woman, "Did God actually say, 'You shall not eat of any tree in the garden'?"

And the woman said to the serpent, "We may eat of the fruit of the trees in the garden, but God said, 'You shall not eat of the fruit of the tree that is in the midst of the garden, neither shall you touch it, lest you die.'"

But the serpent said to the woman, "You will not surely die. For God knows that when you eat of it your eyes will be opened, and you will be like God, knowing good and evil."

So when the woman saw that the tree was good for food, and that it was a delight to the eyes, and that the tree was to be desired to make one wise, she took of its fruit and ate, and she also gave some to her husband who was with her, and he ate. Then the eyes of both were opened, and they knew that they were naked. And they sewed fig leaves together and made themselves loincloths. (Genesis 3:1–7)

At first glance we may not realize how high the stakes are in this encounter. Yet as we read the rest of the Bible and come across phrases like "in Adam we all die,"[1] we realize that however Adam handles this test will result in life or death for the entire human race. And Adam failed miserably. All it took were a few planted seeds of doubt ("did God actually say . . .") about God's intentions toward our first parents and Adam plunged the human race into spiritual ruin.

> All it took were a few planted seeds of doubt and Adam plunged the human race into spiritual ruin.

So whether we like it or not, Adam is our representative. His choice is our choice, and his consequences are our consequences.[2] In one of the saddest pictures in all of Scripture, God drives mankind east of Eden and positions a fierce angel with a flaming sword to keep us out of Paradise.

The damage is now done. Humanity is spiritually dead and separated from God.

WHY REGRET IS THE WORST FEELING

Have you ever noticed that nothing seems to paralyze us like regret? The sad can be comforted. The confused can be enlightened. The angry can be calmed down. But what about the regretful? Until someone invents a time machine so we can go back and reverse events, regret for "what might have been" continues to haunt us. Yet this is

---

1. See 1 Corinthians 15:22.

2. The representative role of Adam over the human race is a neglected doctrine. If we fail to understand it, we will not fully appreciate the great work Jesus has done as our "second Adam." I highly recommend chapter 4, "Adam's Fall and Mine," in R. C. Sproul's book *Chosen by God* (Carol Stream, IL: Tyndale, 1986).

exactly what makes Jesus' showdown with the Devil (the sequel) so amazing. The Son of God totally reverses the damage done by Adam.

The Son of God totally reverses the damage done by Adam.

It is interesting to note that Adam's showdown unfolds in Paradise and leaves mankind in the wilderness. Jesus' confrontation starts in the wilderness in order to get us to paradise. To some it might seem, however, that Adam has the advantage. Adam walks through a lush, beautiful garden. Jesus is led into the lifeless, lonely wilderness. Adam has a full belly. Jesus has not eaten for forty days. Adam has a companion. Jesus is alone.

As the second Adam, Jesus prepares to take His stand against the crafty tempter. Against seemingly impossible odds, Jesus is ready to do what the regretful could never even dream of: to literally change the past.

JESUS SHOWS THAT GOD IS MORE PRECIOUS THAN ANYTHING

It was food—the fruit of the tree of the knowledge of good and evil—that got us into so much trouble in the prequel. So not surprisingly it is food that Satan starts with in the sequel:

And the tempter came and said to him, "If you are the Son of God, command these stones to become loaves of bread."

Most of us become irritable when we miss our morning breakfast, let alone after missing forty of them—along with lunch and supper. And no doubt the One who will soon turn water into wine could easily turn the wilderness into a Panera, couldn't He? But Satan, of course, really has no interest in Jesus' hunger; he is only interested in getting the Messiah's eyes off His Father.

Matthew has already told us that the Spirit of God has led Jesus into the wilderness to go without food until the appropriate time. It is not for Jesus—and especially not for Satan—to determine when that time should be. So the Savior sets the tempter back on his heels.

> "It is written, "'Man shall not live by bread alone, but by every word that comes from the mouth of God.'"

Jesus will live off of God's word—unlike Adam who considered a morsel of fruit more desirable than God's word and promise.

With the Devil's first attempt foiled, he does what any good competitor does: he readjusts. Since Jesus is clinging to God's word, maybe Satan can twist it just enough to throw Him off-balance and send Him (and all of humanity) plummeting to destruction.

> Then the devil took him to the holy city and set him on the pinnacle of the temple and said to him, "If you are the Son of God, throw yourself down, for it is written, "'He will command his angels concerning you,' and "'On their hands they will bear you up, lest you strike your foot against a stone.'"

Satan knows his Deuteronomy, and he knows how to take it out of context. He is trying to get Jesus to "dip into his deity" to show off a little bit. But Jesus knows that now is not the time for His glory to be revealed. Now is the time for humility and hunger. So He out-exposits Satan.

> Jesus said to him, "Again it is written, 'You shall not put the Lord your God to the test.'"

Jesus has one passion: to obey His Father, not test Him. Again, He does what Adam would not.

With no more pretense, Satan makes the only move he has left.

> The devil took him to a very high mountain and showed him
> all the kingdoms of the world and their glory. And he said
> to him, "All these I will give you, if you will fall down and
> worship me."

The Devil is offering Jesus the same thing God the Father has planned for Him: to rule the nations. Yet there is one key difference with Satan's offer—no cross. He's offering Jesus a shortcut if He will just throw a little allegiance the Devil's way. But Jesus has come to do His Father's will—even if it takes Him to the cross. He is done with this menace.

The second Adam has reversed what happened at that first showdown.

> Then Jesus said to him, "Be gone, Satan! For it is
> written, "'You shall worship the Lord your God
> and him only shall you serve.'"

The second Adam has reversed what happened at that first showdown. As our new representative, Jesus has offered the perfect obedience to God that we needed Adam to offer for us. The first major phase of Jesus' mission to destroy the Devil's work is finished.

SATAN'S TRUE MISSION

Have you noticed that when Satan came to do battle with Jesus, he did not hide behind a tree and jump out when Jesus passed by. He didn't bring flies, bleeding walls, or shrieking demons to spook the Son of God. It was no silly caricature in a red satin jumpsuit that met the Messiah in the wilderness. It was the shrewd and crafty fallen angel who used every temptation in his arsenal to get Jesus to choose him over God.

How many times have we failed, when he has tempted us? Countless. But take a moment and thank God for your Savior. He was weak, tired, and hungry. (Did you notice that this showdown left Him so weak that He was in need of the attention of angels?) He stood on the brink of collapse, but He did stand! No longer do we need to be represented by Adam and his path-of-least-resistance choice. No—we have a new hero now, one who considered the word and will of God more precious than anything.

So we have every reason to be filled with hope. In Jesus, Satan has met not just his match, but his superior. And while he may bring everything in his power against us, he cannot contend with our Savior. Again, Luther's famous words ring true.

> And though this world, with devils filled, should threaten to undo us,
> We will not fear, for God hath willed His truth to triumph through us.
> The Prince of Darkness grim, we tremble not for him—
> His rage we can endure, for lo, his doom is sure;
> One little word shall fell him.

QUESTIONS FOR REFLECTION

1. When you think of a famous "showdown," what comes to mind? What were the stakes of the contest?

2. List a few of the similarities between Adam in the garden of Eden and Jesus in the wilderness.

3. Read Matthew 4:1–11. Think about the advantages Adam had over Jesus when facing temptation. How do Jesus' responses to Satan impact the way you think about the Savior?

4. Why do you think the temptation of Jesus is an important story? What does His victory over the Devil mean for you today?

Satan is now a defeated foe, a lion on a chain.
—J. I. PACKER

Those of you who like to see nasty people receive their comeuppance will be delighted with the results of tonight's tale.
—ALFRED HITCHCOCK

Now is the judgment of this world; now will the ruler of this world be cast out.
—JOHN 12:31

CHAPTER FIVE

THE DEVIL'S COMEUPPANCE

Comeuppance. Since childhood this has been one of my favorite words. *Payback, justice, moment of truth*—they all have their place. But none stand out to me like comeuppance. I have even passed on this word to my kids, and it is now guaranteed that whenever we watch some epic Disney movie, one of them will excitedly ask, "Dad, when do you think they'll get their comeuppance?"

In the ongoing battle between good and evil—whether it's on film, in fairy tales, or in thrillers—the evil character is so deplorable, so "punishable," that it seems that the very reason for his presence in the story is to set up a great comeuppance moment. Whether it is Ursula being impaled by a ship, Scar being tossed to the same hungry hyenas he has earlier betrayed, or Gaston falling to the rocks below after his failed attempt on the Beast's life, we love to watch bad guys get what's coming to them. Naturally, then, in a book on Satan, we would ask, "When does the Devil get his comeuppance?"

Of course the most logical guess would be at the end of the story. And there is a comeuppance moment found there.

And the devil who had deceived them was thrown into the lake of fire and sulfur . . . tormented day and night forever and ever. (Revelation 20:10)

What a fitting end for the great adversary of God. The Serpent that slithered through human history for one grand purpose—to keep people out of God's presence forever—finally will be contained in an inescapable prison forever. Never again will he tempt, afflict, or accuse God's people. Satan will be carried out to the eternal landfill and dumped there for all time. In light of this "end of the story," would it surprise you, then, that Jesus says the Devil's comeuppance moment came thousands of years earlier?

> The Serpent slithered through human history for one grand purpose—to keep people out of God's presence forever.

DOES SATAN ACTUALLY RUN THE WORLD?

In John's gospel, Satan is called "the ruler of this world" (John 12:31). Such a powerful title raises an alarming question. Does Satan run the show? Is this *his* world? The thought is troubling on a number of levels. If the Devil is in charge, then how can we ever feel safe in this world? More importantly, what does this say about God's authority and power? When we sing "This Is My Father's World," are we wrong?

Thankfully the Bible does not leave us in the dark on such questions. While it is true that "the whole world lies in the power of the evil one" (1 John 5:19), the phrase "the whole world" has a unique meaning here. John tells us that all that is in the world—"the desires of the flesh and the desires of the eyes and pride in possessions—is not from the Father but is from the world" (1 John 2:16). Thus, pride, evil desires, and base lusts compose the world over which the Devil presides. That is why in the verse just before this description we are commanded, "Do not love the world" (1 John 2:15).

The world that Satan runs is not a reference to plants, people, or places. "Viewed as a people, the world must be loved," writes John Stott. "Viewed as an evil system, organized under the dominion of

Satan not of God, it is not to be loved."[1] There is a kind of environment that exists in the world that is similar to air. We live and breathe in a thoroughly anti-God atmosphere that Satan enjoys managing.

But how did God's wicked adversary come into such a position of power?

Isaiah answers this question, leaving no doubt as to when and how the world that Satan rules came into being.

> "The earth lies defiled under its inhabitants;
>   for they have transgressed the laws,
>   violated the statutes,
>   broken the everlasting covenant.
> Therefore a curse devours the earth,
>   and its inhabitants suffer for their guilt." (Isaiah 24:5–6)

Because mankind has blatantly defied God's law, God himself ordained that "the creation was subjected to futility" (Romans 8:20). In other words, the evil world we inhabit is a world of our own making, and God is allowing Satan to rule it for a temporary period.

This is a profound truth and it is crucial that we understand it: Any power the Devil has is only because God gives it to him for a season. John MacArthur summarizes this well in his book *The Second Coming*:

Any power the Devil has is only because God gives it to him for a season.

> There's a sense in which Satan still runs the world. How did he gain this power? At creation God gave dominion over all creation to Adam. But when Adam succumbed to Satan's enticements, obeying the devil rather than God, Adam in effect abdicated his place of dominion and left

---

1. John Stott, *The Epistles of John*, Tyndale New Testament Commentary (Carol Stream, IL: Tyndale, 1964), 99.

that authority to the devil. Satan has been the ruler of this world ever since. He has no legal right to rule. He's a usurper. Yet God allows him to remain in power."[2]

But one day this usurper's power will be taken away.

THE HOUR HAS COME

Millennia before the day of Satan's comeuppance, whenever that day will be (which only God knows), Jesus made a cosmic announcement: Satan is already finished.

> Now is the judgment of this world; now will the ruler of this world be cast out. (John 12:31)

Jesus speaks of Satan's expulsion from power as something just about to happen, so He could not have been speaking about the Devil's plunge into the lake of fire. The Savior saw something happening in His own ministry that would, in effect, seal the Evil One's doom. Adding to the power of this announcement is the sad and somber tone of Jesus' words just a few sentences earlier: "Now is my soul troubled. And what shall I say? 'Father, save me from this hour'? But for this purpose I have come to this hour" (John 12:27). In a moment of transparent tenderness, He lets us know that He is carrying a tremendous emotional burden—the burden is His "hour."

Throughout John's gospel, Jesus refers to His "hour"—the time of His suffering and death.[3] It hangs over His whole life; He is never unaware of it. In this instance, Jesus has just portrayed His death in heartbreaking imagery: "Truly, truly, I say to you, unless a grain of wheat falls into the earth and dies, it remains alone; but if it dies, it

---

2. John MacArthur, *The Second Coming* (Wheaton, IL: Crossway, 1999), 45.
3. See John 2:4; 4:21, 23; 5:25, 28; 7:8, 30; 8:20; 12:23, 27; 13:1; 17:1.

bears much fruit" (John 12:24). Christ is the *grain of wheat* that will soon perish, and He knows that His *hour* has finally come.

There is something hauntingly sad about the way the term *my hour* or *his hour* is used here. Think about the way we use that word today. An Olympic runner who comes from behind and surges to victory in the last moment is said to have had her "finest hour." Parents sit in a concert hall and fight back tears as the audience around them is spellbound by the pianist's skills. Mom and Dad have known the exceptional talent of their son, but now the world sees it; it is his "finest hour." For us "the hour" is the moment of success, fame, or hard-earned recognition. For Jesus it was the moment of His suffering, death, and rejection.

Who would ever expect an announcement of victory in such a sad context? Yet even though His soul is troubled, even though He must now face an unimaginable period of torture and pain, Jesus issues the declaration: "Now is the judgment of this world; now will the ruler of this world be cast out" (John 12:31).

> Satan feared such a turn of events and used every weapon in his arsenal to keep it from happening.

Jesus understands that the cross will topple Satan from his throne of power. Satan feared such a turn of events and used every weapon in his arsenal to keep it from happening.

SATAN DID NOT WANT JESUS TO GO TO THE CROSS

As a young Christian I was taught that the Devil wanted Jesus to be crucified, that he delighted on the day his wish came true, and that Satan and all of his minions celebrated from Friday through early Sunday morning when their party was crashed by Jesus' resurrection. This view is popular, and in one of my favorite sermons, it is prominently displayed. Tony Campolo's famous sermon, "It's Friday, But Sunday's Coming," is a wonderful message. It beautifully captures the contrast between the gloomy sadness of Good Friday and the euphoric joy of Easter Sunday. Yet one line troubles me. "It's Friday. Jesus is hanging on the cross, heaven is weeping and hell is partying. But that's because it's Friday, and they don't know it, but Sunday's a coming." This line troubles me because the picture of Satan partying seems far removed from what we find in Scripture.

Consider the moment when Jesus first tells His disciples that He is going to Jerusalem to be crucified. "From that time Jesus began to show his disciples that he must go to Jerusalem and suffer many things from the elders and chief priests and scribes, and be killed, and on the third day be raised" (Matthew 16:21).

Such a grim destiny does not sit well with Peter. After all, he has given up everything to follow Jesus—his family, his business, his comfortable routine. He has given up everything to follow a Messiah who is going to die?

No, Peter will have none of this, and he decides to talk some sense into his friend. "Peter took [Jesus] aside and began to rebuke him, saying, 'Far be it from you, Lord! This shall never happen to you'" (Matthew 16:22).

Before we are too tough on Peter, however, let's look at it from his perspective. Isn't he simply trying to act the way any good friend would? Imagine a dear friend telling you he is taking a trip to a place where he knows a bloodthirsty crowd is waiting to kill him. What kind of a friend would you be if you didn't try to stop him? Peter's expression is the natural, loving reaction of a good friend. Yet Jesus sees it as pure evil.

How stunned Peter must have been when Jesus turned to him and sternly said, "Get behind me, Satan! You are a hindrance to me. For you are not setting your mind on the things of God, but on the things of man" (Matthew 16:23).

Without realizing it, the fisherman-turned-apostle has just become Satan's mouthpiece. The Devil is using Peter's well-intentioned words as a roadblock to the cross. Why? Because Satan was terrified of Jesus going to the cross.

THE CROSS IS THE DEATH BLOW—HELL IS THE PAPERWORK

Now we can appreciate the proclamation of "the ruler of this world" being "cast out." Jesus saw His death looming large in the hours before Him; and while it would be vicious in its brutality, He could see through to the victory. It would be *His hour* that finally brought *Satan's hour* to an end.

The apostle Paul makes this point clear when he says that Jesus "disarmed the rulers and authorities and put them to open shame, by triumphing over them" (Colossians 2:15). The "rulers and authorities" are those demonic forces that get their comeuppance at the cross. Paul's words paint a picture of a great military general whose valor in battle has secured a great victory for his people. Now he marches these enemy soldiers forth as prisoners of war to be openly mocked and ridiculed.

"The Lord Jesus Christ has done everything for his people, fought their battle, won their victory, and, on their behalf, celebrated the triumph in the streets of heaven, 'leading captivity captive.' What more, then, do we want? Surely Christ is enough for us."[4]

Satan's final destruction—being thrown into the fiery lake—is something we can eagerly await. But Jesus has already secured the victory, striking the deathblow to the Devil and his dominion by

---

4. C. H. Spurgeon, "Death and Its Sentence Abolished," The Spurgeon Archive, http://www.spurgeon.org/sermons/2605.htm, accessed on December 2, 2010.

going to the cross. In many ways, Satan's swan dive into hell is just the final filing of the paperwork.

Many see the cross as a temporary setback and the resurrection as the delayed victory. But the significance of the resurrection is that it confirms the soul-saving, Satan-crushing work of the cross. John Stott says it concisely: "The cross was the victory won, and the resurrection the victory endorsed, proclaimed and demonstrated."[5]

Like the resurrection, the final punishment of our enemy just confirms the success of the cross. So while we must endure the Devil's activities for now, we are facing an enemy who is already mortally wounded. Imagine that you were told you were going to have to fight the heavyweight champion of the world just one hour from now. If you're like me you have already determined that there is no point doing pushups, so you resolve to eat your bag of potato chips and make sure your medical insurance card is up to date. Just as you get off the couch to prepare for your inevitable beat down, your phone rings. "He is going to be there, but he is in chains and under police escort," the voice on the other end tells you. Suddenly your confidence changes, not because you have beefed up like a muscle-covered jock in an infomercial, but because your enemy is no longer in the uncontested position of power. This is what our Savior has done to Satan by dying on the cross for us.

> While we must endure the Devil's activities for now, we are facing an enemy who is already mortally wounded.

In the next chapter we will consider just why the cross was able to bring about the Devil's destruction. But for now, let's just revel in it:

> Christ's cross spoils Satan of his universal monarchy. He could once lord it over the whole world and he does very

---

5. John Stott, *The Cross of Christ* (Downers Grove, IL: InterVarsity, 2006), 231.

much of that even now, but there is a people over whom he cannot sway his evil scepter! There is a race which has broken loose from him. They are free and they defy him to enslave them again. They care not for his threats, they are not to be won by his enticements, and though he worries and tempts them, yet he cannot destroy them—he can boast no longer of universal dominion! There is a Seed of the woman that has revolted from him, for Jesus, by His death, has redeemed them out of the hand of the enemy and they are free![6]

QUESTIONS FOR REFLECTION

1. Do you have a favorite "comeuppance moment" from a book or movie for a particularly nasty villain? Why do you think we like these kind of scenes so much?

2. Read John 12:31. In your own words explain these statements: a) "God is in charge of the world," and b) "Satan is in charge of the world."

3. Consider this quote from this chapter: "For us 'the hour' is the moment of success, fame, or hard-earned recognition. For Jesus it was the moment of His suffering, death, and rejection." How does reflecting upon this idea of "Jesus' hour" affect your love and appreciation for Christ?

4. Read Matthew 16:23. Do you agree that this verse is sufficient proof that Satan did not want Jesus to go to the cross? Why do you think it is hard for some Christians to see Good Friday as the moment of Jesus' decisive victory?

5. The focus of the next chapter is on why the cross is the moment of Satan's comeuppance. Before reading it, however, why do you think Jesus' death is the moment when the Devil was defeated?

---

6. Spurgeon, "Death and Its Sentence."

It's the end of the world as we know it, and I feel fine.
—R.E.M.

You're gonna fit right in. Everyone in here is innocent.
—RED, *THE SHAWSHANK REDEMPTION*

There is therefore now no condemnation for those who are in Christ Jesus.
—ROMANS 8:1

CHAPTER SIX

THE END OF THE WORLD IN THE HERE AND NOW

Years ago the group R.E.M. had a hit song called "The End of the World as We Know It." Part of the attraction of the song was the fusion of its serious and somber title with a catchy, lighthearted beat. The last line of the chorus cleverly brings these seemingly incompatible themes together: "It's the end of the world as we know it, and I feel fine."

Of course what works well in rock music falls apart if we try to take the same approach with the end of the world as described in the Bible. It is hard to "feel fine" when reading about outpoured wrath, plagues, cosmic upheaval, and the final judgment of all things evil. No, the end of the world seems far removed from the humdrum nature of everyday life. But what if the end is closer than we think?

As we saw in the last chapter, Satan was defeated—something we would expect to happen at the end of history—at the moment of Christ's crucifixion. So are there other anticipated end-of-the-world events that have already occurred? Think about this: When does God issue His verdict of where we will spend eternity? Immediately our minds may go to the book of Revelation again. There we see God judging all the people who have ever lived and sentencing them to heaven or hell. Yet a closer examination of Scripture shows that for some people, at least, that verdict comes much sooner.

EACH HUMAN LIFE IS A COURT CASE

We have already considered Satan as a gleeful prosecutor. With dogged determination he accuses every person who has ever lived, day and night, before the bench of God's justice. And while he is a brilliant prosecutor who is able to (and does) whip up lies and fabrications about the sin in our lives, he does not need to. Each human life furnishes enough evidence about man's sinful condition to fill the accuser's legal pad from cover to cover. Just as he stood before Joshua, the high priest, and pointed at his dirty clothes, so does he stand before each of us and point out our unworthiness before a holy and righteous God.

He wants to hear a resounding "Guilty!" echo through the chambers of eternity.

What is the Devil waiting for? God's verdict. He wants to hear a resounding "Guilty!" echo through the chambers of eternity. So it is not just a figurative expression to say that every human life is a prolonged court case.

We are on trial. We are being prosecuted. And God will certainly issue a verdict over every person who has ever lived.

And the terrible truth is: We are guilty. "None is righteous, no, not one" (Romans 3:10). As David reminds us, we were conceived in sin (Psalm 51:5). We are doomed right from the start. The rest of our childhood, adolescence, and adulthood are just further accumulations of charges against us. As the apostle Paul writes, "Because of your hard and impenitent heart *you are storing up wrath for yourself* on the day of wrath when God's righteous judgment will be revealed" (Romans 2:5, emphasis added). Satan must delight as he amasses more and more evidence of our guilt before God.

When the verdict is issued, it will be final. There is no court more supreme than the throne of God's perfect justice.

Is there any way to stop this persistent prosecutor? Can that legal pad be ripped from his hands forever? If only he could be driven out!

Wait! Isn't that what we discussed in the last chapter?

WHY THE CROSS DRIVES SATAN OUT

In my fifteen years as a pastor, I have noticed that most Christians will say that Jesus' death on the cross has rescued them. It seems that few, however, can really say why. Even believing children will utter the statement, "Jesus died for my sins." But as we mature, we should be able to explain why His death takes care of our sin problem.

To get some help with this, let's go back to the story of Joshua, the high priest, standing before God and Satan in dirty clothes.

> "Then he showed me Joshua the high priest standing before the angel of the LORD, and Satan standing at his right hand to accuse him." (Zechariah 3:1)

This is a vision given to the prophet Zechariah by God. What is interesting is that the scene would look different to Joshua himself. As high priest, Joshua is just doing one of his many priestly duties in the temple, serving the people of Israel as their high priest. It is doubtful that he sees what the prophet sees in the vision. It is as if Zechariah can see into the invisible realm, and there, in high definition clarity, is the prosecutor doing what he does best—accusing one of God's servants. The Devil has a solid case too, as Zechariah indicates:

> "Now Joshua was standing before the angel, clothed with filthy garments." (3:3)

In the original Hebrew language the wording here means that Joshua's clothing is covered in animal excrement. In our

Purel-sanitized culture, that picture is disturbing for sanitary reasons. In Joshua's time, however, it was a much bigger deal. The priest's clothing would have been considered ceremonially unclean, and in that condition, Joshua had no business standing in God's presence.

What a picture of humanity in our exposed, deplorable condition before God. Isaiah uses this same metaphor when he writes, "We have all become like one who is unclean, and all our righteous deeds are like a polluted garment" (Isaiah 64:6).

Imagine a child playing waist-deep in a huge mud puddle. Ask him to clean himself up and to remove the caked-on mud from his skin. He tries to wipe his mud-encrusted hand on his mud-encrusted cheek, but only succeeds in transferring filth from one area of his body to another. Unless that child gets outside help from someone with soap and a few buckets of water, he is not going to get clean. The same holds true for Joshua in his filthy garments, There is nothing Joshua can do about his own uncleanness since he is already contaminated (and the same holds true for us in our sinful condition). Unless the high priest gets outside help, he is vulnerable to Satan's accusations. And the divine Helper comes to his rescue.

> And the Lord said to Satan, "The LORD rebuke you, O Satan!
> The LORD who has chosen Jerusalem rebuke you! Is not this
> a brand plucked from the fire?" (Zechariah 3:2)

Joshua can do nothing about his problem, but God can. In fact, God has "plucked him from the fire." This means that God has chosen to save this unworthy servant so he is exempt from Satan's accusations. As we read further we see why.

> And the angel said to those who were standing before him,
> "Remove the filthy garments from him." And to him he said,

"Behold, I have taken your iniquity away from you, and I will clothe you with pure vestments." (Zechariah 3:4)

In saving Joshua, God solves both of the priest's problems: 1) He removes his filthy clothes; and 2) He provides clean clothes that are acceptable to God. This whole passage is a foreshadowing of, and preparation for, the work that Jesus would do centuries later.

The place where God takes away our filth and gives us righteousness is the cross. "For our sake he made him to be sin who knew no sin, so that in him we might become the righteousness of God" (2 Corinthians 5:21). This succinct passage speaks of an exchange. God graciously exchanges our sin for Christ's righteousness. To put it another way, Jesus takes all of our dirty clothes (our filth, our sin, our rebellion), and He gives us His clean clothes (His righteousness, His moral perfection, His obedience). There is a reason the word *gospel* means "good news"!

SO WHAT HAPPENS TO SATAN'S LEGAL PAD?

Jesus does what we could never do for ourselves. He snatches away Satan's legal pad and in its place hands him a new page with your name at the top. The former was an endless list of sins, any one of which was sufficient to seal your eternal misery. The second is brief and easy for the gleeful prosecutor to read. It simply says "the perfect, flawless obedience of Jesus Christ." Case closed.

Once Jesus takes our moral guilt upon himself, Satan is left speechless. As John Piper writes, "If the death of Jesus takes away the condemning power of our sin, then the chief weapon of the devil is taken out of his hand.

> "If the death of Jesus takes away the condemning power of our sin, then the chief weapon of the devil is taken out of his hand."
>
> —JOHN PIPER

He cannot make a case for our death penalty, because the Judge has acquitted us by the death of his Son!"

Do you see why Satan influenced Peter and tried to keep Jesus from making it to the cross? He knew full well that the day Jesus died would be the day of his comeuppance.

We can now ask how this interruption of the Devil's closing argument impacts that fearful verdict that we would expect on judgment day and how that future verdict can be brought into the present. This is when we turn to what many consider the greatest verse in the whole Bible.

THE VERDICT: "NO CONDEMNATION"

> There is therefore now no condemnation for those who are in Christ Jesus. (Romans 8:1)

One of the reasons this verse is the favorite of so many is that they recognize it for what it is: a verdict. And do you notice the timing of it? Now! "There is therefore *now* no condemnation for those who are in Christ Jesus." The verdict that would have otherwise been issued on that terrible day of judgment can be brought into the present, and it is good!

No more suspense, wondering and waiting for the verdict in the final scene. God has issued His verdict: no condemnation, not guilty, free from Satan's accusations. This is what happened when Jesus took away our sin by dying on the cross.

"No condemnation." In the remaining chapters we will explore the amazing implications of this verdict. If the enemy of our souls has lost his chief weapon against us, then we are free to live a totally different kind of life. Yet many Christians do not enjoy the benefits Jesus has secured for them—perhaps the greatest benefit being freedom from guilt.

Bishop Robert South once wrote, "Guilt upon the conscience, like rust upon iron, both defiles and consumes it, gnawing and creeping into it, as that does which at last eats out the very heart and substance of the metal." What a tragic way for freed prisoners to live.

If you have ever struggled with guilt over your sin, let me invite you to meditate on Romans 8:1: "There is therefore now *no condemnation* for those who are in Christ Jesus." So many sincere believers live as though that verse says "there is now only *a tiny bit of condemnation* for those who are in Christ Jesus." They accept that God has forgiven them, and they can see how Jesus' death has paid their penalty, but they can't quite bring themselves to believe that there is *zero guilt* left before God. Yet the verdict God issues is emphatic. "No Condemnation" should be shouted from the rooftops.

The late F. F. Bruce put it well: "There is no reason why those who are in Christ Jesus should go on doing penal servitude as though they had never been pardoned and liberated from the prison house of sin."[1]

We are free from Satan's accusations. But this does not mean that he actually stops accusing us. On the contrary, it seems as if he works even harder at getting us to believe that we are not free. And at times he is very effective, because we can still find ourselves battling guilt and despair into the wee hours of an especially dark morning. Then, more than ever, we would be wise to follow the example of Charles Spurgeon when the Devil came knocking on his door.

When Satan accuses, Christ pleads. He does not wait until the case has gone against us and then express his

---

1. As quoted in R. Kent Hughes, *Romans: Righteousness from Heaven* (Wheaton, IL: Crossway, 1991), 148.

regret, but he is always a very present help in time of trouble. He knows the heart of Satan, being omniscient God, and long before Satan can accuse he puts in the demurrer [objection], the blessed plea on our behalf, and stays the sentence until he gives an answer which silences for ever every accusation. Do not think, Christian, that there will ever come a night so dark that there will be no light shining for you in it, or that Satan will be able to surprise the Saviour and take you by storm. At the nick of time Christ will be sure to be your help.

QUESTIONS FOR REFLECTION

1. Think of an intense scene in a movie or TV show involving the anticipation of a jury's verdict. Why do you think such scenes are so suspenseful? How do you think people would be impacted if they actually believed that their lives will end in a final verdict from God?

2. Read 2 Corinthians 5:21. Some have called this verse the most succinct statement of the gospel anywhere in Scripture. Write a paraphrase of this verse in your own words.

3. Piper writes, "If the death of Jesus takes away the condemning power of our sin, then the chief weapon of the devil is taken out of his hand. He cannot make a case for our death penalty, because the Judge has acquitted us by the death of his Son!" How could the truth of this statement be used to help someone struggling with guilt and shame?

4. Read Romans 8:1. This passage boldly issues a verdict of "no condemnation." Why is it so difficult for people to live in this reality? What do you think is the secret to consistently living in this kind of freedom?

PART THREE

SATAN, I DEFY YOU!

We confide in our strength, without boasting of it; we respect that of others, without fearing it.

—THOMAS JEFFERSON

Conceit, more rich in matter than in words, brags of his substance: they are but beggars who can count their worth.

—WILLIAM SHAKESPEARE

And the king of Israel answered, "Tell him, 'Let not him who straps on his armor boast himself like he who takes it off.'"

—1 KINGS 20:11

CHAPTER SEVEN

AM I ALLOWED TO MOCK THE DEVIL?

They hunkered down in the craft supply closet and prepared to do battle with Satan. It was 1987 and they had the mullets and "Lord's Gym" T-shirts to prove it. To uninformed outsiders they probably looked like two teenage nerds about to do a sub-par job teaching second graders in Vacation Bible School. To the enlightened, they were warriors of truth who were about to vanquish Satan and all of his hellish minions!

These two pimple-faced heroes paced the oversized closet with their eyes closed tightly and their fists clenched like boxers. Wimps prayed sitting down, but demon-slayers like these guys needed to walk while they prayed. If you can call what they did prayer. They called out threats like "Satan, you are a wimp! You don't have the guts to show yourself to us, do you?" Or, "Devil—you are so afraid of us that you are trembling right now, aren't you? Admit it!" Using the name of Jesus like a machine gun, they blew holes into unseen demons.

What never really dawned on these guys, however, was that they seemed to talk more to Satan than to God when they prayed.

How do I know all this? Because I was one of those guys. Matt was the other one—a young man who loved the Lord and led me, his peer, to Christ when I was sixteen. We were largely on our own, with little or no spiritual mentoring for those first few years after my conversion, influenced by a bizarre combination of TV evangelists, Christian rock music, and cheesy gospel movies from the early 1970s.

Today Matt and I laugh often about those formative years and how God, in His grace, allowed us to make total fools of ourselves in the slow process of growing us up. Looking back we also ask ourselves what God thought of our taunting words to the Devil.

SATAN, I DEFY YOU!

My original title for this book, "Satan, I Defy You," was taken from a line in the hymn "Jesus, Priceless Treasure," which I shared in chapter one. The publisher chose a better title; I will happily concede that. But the "demon hunting" Matt and I engaged in as teens seems to fit quite nicely with "Satan, I Defy You," doesn't it? After all, that is exactly what we were doing—defying the loathsome Satan.

And we weren't alone. Many Christians taunt, mock, and ridicule the Devil. A few months ago, I saw a church sign that said "Want To Kick the Devil's Backside? Come On In!" The sign made me wonder if Satan was making a personal appearance there that Sunday!

Let's consider a rarely discussed passage that seems like the perfect setup to Devil backside kicking. Jude only wrote one book in the New Testament, and it has only one chapter. Nevertheless, he left us with a doozy of a passage.

> Yet in like manner these people also, relying on their dreams, defile the flesh, reject authority, and blaspheme the glorious ones. But when the archangel Michael, contending with the devil, was disputing about the body of Moses, he did not presume to pronounce a blasphemous judgment, but said, "The Lord rebuke you." But these people blaspheme all that they do not understand, and they are destroyed by all that they, like unreasoning animals, understand instinctively. (Jude 1:8–10)

This is a textbook example of an obscure passage. Satan and Michael fighting over Moses' body? Where is *that* in the Old Testament? When was the last time you heard a sermon on this text? But if we get too caught up in the *obscurity* of the passage rather than the *point* of the passage, we will miss an amazing insight. So for the moment, let's just accept the account at face value.

We have walked into a dispute between Satan and Michael the archangel. This is not just an exchange of words. They are "contending"—which in a rather understated way is saying that this is a cosmic battle between two supernatural powerhouses.

Of particular interest is the fact that Michael isn't just a run-of-the-mill angel; he is the archangel, the Optimus Prime of angels (for you Transformer fans). Many commentators even suggest that Satan once held Michael's position, heightening the rivalry to fever pitch level. And think of how powerful Michael must be. Consider that in one Old Testament episode just one angel killed 185,000 Assyrian soldiers in the span of one night (2 Kings 19:35).

So here we have the highest-ranking commander in God's angelic army, ready to do battle against His greatest opponent. Jude has set up the audience for a battle royal. Before we can even grab our popcorn, however, the scene seems to fizzle out.

IS MICHAEL AFRAID OF SATAN?

If there was some kind of battle, Jude doesn't tell us about it. He simply records that the archangel Michael said to the Devil, "The Lord rebuke you." That's it? Michael doesn't even tap into his own fierce, angelic strength to make the threat. He simply points upward and attributes the rebuke to God. That's right. And this is exactly the point Jude wants us to see.

In the previous verses he refers to depraved people who "reject authority, and blaspheme the glorious ones." These appear to be a group of charlatans who are exploiting the early Christian community for their selfish ambitions. They are self-appointed spiritual experts who care about nothing but themselves. They have no respect for any authority and apparently make mocking comments about spiritual beings (whether angels, demons, or both we can't be sure). Having such an exaggerated sense of self-importance, they are cavalier in their approach to the spiritual realm. Jude wants us to see the contrast between these sleazy characters and a true servant of God, Michael.

Michael has a healthy respect for the seriousness of standing against a creature as powerful as Satan. "But when the archangel Michael, contending with the devil, was disputing about the body of Moses, he did not *presume* to pronounce a blasphemous judgment." He did not presume. This is the key difference between someone who truly understands spiritual warfare and the swaggering demon hunters who think the whole thing is like a cool action movie. Matt and I, in our teenage brashness, had no clue how silly we were being. Today we marvel at God's patience and grace with us. "Can you imagine," we ask each other, "if God had pulled back the veil and allowed us to see the creature we were taunting?"

Michael the archangel is not afraid to confront Satan, but he will not do so in his own power. The battle is the Lord's, and Michael relies solely on God's strength and authority when squaring off with the Devil.

High-fiving each other while trash-talking Satan may be fun, but it is anything but wise. If Michael, in all of his supernatural authority and strength, was not cavalier or presumptuous in his approach to Satan, then how much more should weak, feeble sinners like us be humble in our handling of such things?

SO IS IT WRONG TO DEFY SATAN?

Considering Michael's example, then, should we ever say "Satan, I defy you"? Maybe we could say, "Satan, the Lord defy you," or something close to it? After all, we want to be humble and cautious in our approach to the spiritual realm. Yet I want to suggest that we can say "Satan, I defy you"—if we do it in the right way. So sometimes the answer is yes and sometimes it is no. Don't you hate that?

We can say "Satan, I defy you"—if we do it in the right way.

Words have meaning according to their context, right? For instance, consider the sentence "Show me your driver's license, please." If you are like most people, your mind has already supplied a context. Chances are your brain has already put those words in the mouth of a towering police officer, leaning into your driver's side window and glaring at you through his mirrored sunglasses. The request for your license has ignited an explosion of goose bumps on your flesh as you desperately (and silently, of course) pray, "Oh, please let it just be a warning, Lord." Yet I never said anything about speeding, or the highway patrol, or that you were even in a vehicle. Your mind did all that for you.

Now imagine you are standing at your front door in your pajamas. The prize patrol has interrupted your morning coffee, and your jaw hangs open as you stare at a billboard-size check with two entries: ten million dollars and your name. Suddenly, "Show me your driver's license, please" is an invitation to verify that you are the legal recipient of that check.

Context is everything. And that is true with spiritual things as well.

The remaining chapters of this book have bold, in-your-face titles: "Satan, You're Wrong!" "Satan, You Don't Scare Me!" "Satan, You're Fired!" and "Satan, You Disgust Me!" I believe that it is our privilege as forgiven and freed sinners to utter such things *in the right context*. If we walk with a swagger in our step and foolish pride in our hearts, then such statements are anything but helpful; in fact, they are probably quite harmful to us (and others) spiritually. If we think we have some kind of internal power, or the self-appointed right to trash-talk the Devil, we are in danger of relying on our own strength—and how far will that get us in a supernatural battle? Yet if we are biblically grounded, we can make such verbal thrusts with joy and confidence.

When the apostle Paul prepared to preach the gospel, he put no confidence in his oratory skills, intellect, or ability to persuade. Knowing that a person cannot be impressed, reasoned, or persuaded into the kingdom of God, he put all his hope in God's power. This is why Paul said, "My speech and my message were not in plausible words of wisdom, but in demonstration of the Spirit and of power, that your faith might not rest in the wisdom of men but in the power of God" (1 Corinthians 2:4–5). Yet just a few chapters later we find him saying, "To the weak I became weak, that *I might win* the weak. I have become all things to all people, that by all means *I might save* some" (1 Corinthians 9:22, emphasis added).

Knowing that a person cannot be impressed, reasoned, or persuaded into the kingdom of God, he put all his hope in God's power.

What? Doesn't Paul know that he cannot save anyone? Only God's power can do that. Of course he knows that. Paul is just using good theological shorthand. He can say "*I might save* some," knowing full well that he is merely the instrument through which God's power will flow.

Years ago I was leading a meeting where we were brainstorming about creative ways to reach our community for Christ. I started the meeting by saying, "We must make it our priority to make disciples." A well-intentioned man raised his hand and rose to his feet. Clearing his throat, he opined, "I would just like to remind everyone here that we don't make disciples. Only the Holy Spirit does." Then he sat down with that smile that all theological police show when they've saved the church from falling into rank heresy. I chose not to respond in kind by telling him that Jesus himself commanded us to "Go therefore and make disciples" (Matthew 28:19). Had even Jesus forgotten that we cannot make disciples ourselves? How ridiculous! No, we have the freedom to speak a kind of biblical shorthand when we pray, preach, and converse with each other.

So I now invite you to say, "Satan, I defy you!", understanding that only in the authority and power of Jesus is this possible. We would be hopelessly at the Devil's mercy (of which he is woefully lacking) were it not for our Savior. Yet because of what Jesus has done in defeating the Prince of Darkness, we are free. We are free to defy Satan, to decry him, to reject him.

By the grace and power of Jesus, let's do just that!

QUESTIONS FOR REFLECTION

1. Have you seen examples of people getting a bit too carried away with "hunting down" Satan? Do you think this behavior is silly or may even have the potential to be harmful? Why?

2. Read Jude 8–10. How should Michael's response to the Devil impact our own response to the Devil?

3. Do you think it is acceptable to say, "Satan, I defy you?" Why or why not?

4. "Make disciples" is a shorthand way of saying "the Holy Spirit makes disciples through you." "Win some" is a shorthand way of saying "God, working through me, will win people to Christ." So what does it mean to say, "Satan, I defy you?"

My dogs are barking today.

—DEL GRIFFITH IN
PLANES, TRAINS AND AUTOMOBILES

Do not be bullied out of your common sense by the
specialist; two to one, he is a pedant.

—OLIVER WENDELL HOLMES

In your light do we see light.

—PSALM 36:9

CHAPTER EIGHT

SATAN, YOU'RE WRONG!

Satan's doom is sealed, but he has not surrendered. Jesus' death on the cross has won the victory, but the Devil will not give up. His eternal destiny is the lake of fire, but he will not stop scheming.

"Satan has at one point at least lost his grip on reality," writes J. I. Packer. "There is a maggot in his brain we might say, which compels him to deny that he is a captive and beaten foe and to believe that if he fights hard enough against God and God's children he will overthrow them in the end."[1]

So while the Bible certainly celebrates Satan's downfall, it never dismisses him or his ability to have a negative impact on the life of the Christian. A foe that won't stop fighting, exploiting any opportunity to do harm, has to be taken seriously. Our enemy has not let God's verdict of "no condemnation" stop him from making his relentless arguments against our sin and unworthiness. There is a good reason he is called "the accuser of the *brothers*"—that is, the redeemed, forgiven children of God.

> A foe that won't stop fighting, exploiting any opportunity to do harm, has to be taken seriously.

---

1. J. I. Packer, *God's Words* (Downers Grove, IL: InterVarsity, 1981), 83.

"But what harm can he do anymore?" you might ask. "We are freed from God's deserved judgment, right?" Free from God's wrath—indeed! Free from harm—no way!

STICKS AND STONES ARE NOTHING!

Years ago I heard a fiery young youth pastor preach an equally fiery sermon called "The Devil Can Bark, But He Can't Bite!" The students laughed, cried, and hung on his every word.

"Satan is a chained dog," he shouted.

And he is.

"The devil can no longer bite us with the power of death and condemnation," he railed.

And he cannot.

"The devil can only bark, bark, bark, like a whipped puppy," he blared.

So true.

"And that bark of his can't hurt us one bit," he concluded.

So wrong!

Whoever invented the phrase "Sticks and stones may break my bones, but words will never hurt me" was apparently unaware of what the Bible has to say about the power of the tongue and words.

Death and life are in the power of the tongue, and those who love it will eat its fruits. (Proverbs 18:21)

A soft answer turns away wrath, but a harsh word stirs up anger. (Proverbs 15:1)

So also the tongue is a small member, yet it boasts of great things. How great a forest is set ablaze by such a small fire! (James 3:5)

Words are extremely powerful. Words can literally change a person's life. They have the power to tear people to pieces or fortify them with strength and hope.

Words also carry the power of ideas; and ideas can change the world. In the 1800s a young physician named Ignaz Philipp Semmelweiss had the *idea* that unwashed hands might be to blame for an absurdly high infant mortality rate. Centuries later, millions of lives that never would have gotten past infancy have that Viennese doctor to thank. Steve Jobs had an *idea* about having "a thousand songs in your pocket" and millions of iPods later, you're totally unhip if you don't own one.

Sadly, however, not all ideas lead to happy endings.

Shortly after World War I, a young German corporal was recovering in a Berlin hospital and was infected with an *idea*: Jews were responsible for Germany's defeat and humiliation. Adolf Hitler went on to slaughter millions of people, fueled by his twisted idea.

Satan masters words because they are the building blocks of ideas, and ideas have power. He plots, prepares, and ambushes with words, hoping they will destroy countless lives. He can bark—and he can bite!

SATAN'S FAVORITE BARKS

The evidence of Satan's handiwork is all around us. Satan's words are not all-powerful, but they can still do damage. How many friendships, marriages, and churches are crippled by the Devil's assaults? It appears that he has developed a few simple ideas, and more importantly, he has mastered the art of selling them.

> Satan's words are not all-powerful, but they can still do damage.

Yet just imagine if we were always on our guard, if we were not fooled by Satan's trick plays. As we saw in chapter two, that is exactly the stance the Bible tells us to take. We are the ones who "would not be out-witted by Satan, for we are not ignorant of his designs" (2 Corinthians 2:11). Not his pitchfork or his hooves, but his *designs*, the well-thought-out ideas and strategies that would trip us up. This is why the apostle Paul warns us to be on high-alert level: "See to it that no one takes you captive by philosophy and empty deceit, according to human tradition" (Colossians 2:8). Philosophy, deceit, seductive ideas—these are Satan's "barks" and they have immense power. While we could spend the rest of this book considering the specific thoughts he seeks to implant in our minds, let's just concentrate on three: guilt, pleasure, and self-justification.

BARK #1: GUILT

If Satan were allowed only one weapon, I am convinced that guilt would be his choice. After all, he is "the accuser," and guilt is the basis of accusation. No one is ever accused of being innocent. Yet one would think that Satan would be silenced for-

If Satan were allowed only one weapon, guilt would be his choice.

ever when seeking to accuse a believer in Jesus Christ. Because of the death of Jesus for sinners, the Christian enjoys an irrevocable "no condemnation" status before God, and there is no doubt that the Devil hates this truth. Yet he has figured out that Christians can still *feel* guilty, and he will happily exploit that feeling.

The taunts may vary slightly, but they are essentially the same bark:

> "You have no right to publicly pray in church. You are a bitter, angry person, and God would never want you to be heard."
> "Ha! You don't deserve that good man as your husband; you had an abortion as a teenager."
> "What? Don't you dare step into that pulpit; you are nothing but a pathetic hypocrite."

On and on the bully heckles, *bark, bark, bark! Guilty, guilty, guilty!* Guilt soon leads to paralysis, and an immobile believer cannot make the kind of dynamic, spiritual impact on the world that God desires. Therefore we must be ready to laugh at these taunts, and throw them right back in the Devil's face: "Satan, you're wrong."

Martin Luther was a man who struggled mightily with guilt throughout his early life. After becoming a monk, he threw himself into a vigorous, self-punishing process, trying to purge his guilt through human effort. He once said, "If ever a monk got to heaven by his 'monkery,' I was that monk!" Then one day he discovered the truth that God pronounces His verdict of "not guilty" over all who trust in Jesus. Luther, however, soon learned that Satan did not lessen his attacks on his conscience. So rattled was the young monk-turned-reformer by the Devil's jeers that he once threw a bottle of ink at the wall near his desk.

Fortunately, Luther learned how to combat Satan by turning the accuser's own words against him. It was his joy to teach us how to do the same.

> When the devil tells us we are sinners and therefore damned, we may answer, "Because you say I am a sinner, I will be righteous and saved."
>
> Then the devil will say, "No, you will be damned."
>
> And I will reply, "No, for I fly to Christ who has given himself for my sins. Therefore, Satan, you will not prevail against me when you try to terrify me by telling me how great my sins are and try to reduce me to heaviness, distrust, despair, hatred, contempt, and blasphemy. On the contrary, when you say I am a sinner, you give me armor and weapons against yourself, so that I can cut your throat with your own sword and tread you under my feet, for Christ died for sinners. . . . Whenever you object that I

am a sinner, you remind me of the benefit of Christ my Redeemer. It is on his shoulders, not mine, that all my sins lie. . . . So when you say I am a sinner, you do not terrify me but comfort me immeasurably."[2]

What a wonderful tactic to employ! Like Luther we too can say, "That's right, Devil, tell me what a vile sinner I am. It will simply make me see more of Jesus, who bore my sin in my place and removed it far from me."

Too many Christians believe the lie that Satan paints with his wicked words. They forget that God has forever absolved them from the guilt of sin. The way out of this trap is simple: tell Satan your testimony. God has fully pardoned you of your sin, and you can tell the Devil to pack up his bag of guilt and leave.

BARK #2: PLEASURE

It has been observed that if we could see sin for what it really is, we would run for the hills when we see it. Then why do we embrace it so often and with so much passion? Because Satan is a brilliant salesman; he can make trash look like treasure and a poison pill taste like a Popsicle. This shouldn't surprise us, since he has been perfecting his persuasive craft from the moment the first human ever set foot on the planet.

Let's revisit the garden of Eden again. Remember how Satan came to Eve, the mother of us all?

> Now the serpent was more crafty than any other beast of the field that the LORD God had made.
>
> He said to the woman, "Did God actually say, 'You shall not eat of any tree in the garden'?" And the woman said to the serpent, "We may eat of the fruit of the trees in the garden, but

---

2. Martin Luther, *Galatians* (Wheaton, IL: Crossway, 1998), 40–41.

God said, 'You shall not eat of the fruit of the tree that is in the midst of the garden, neither shall you touch it, lest you die.'"

But the serpent said to the woman, "You will not surely die. For God knows that when you eat of it your eyes will be opened, and you will be like God, knowing good and evil." (Genesis 3:1–5)

Think about Eve's situation. She lives in a perfect paradise, has a perfect husband (how often can you say that and literally mean it?), and most importantly, she wakes up every morning to the glory and beauty of God. Advertisers like to flirt with the question "What do you give to the woman who has everything?" Never has this been truer of any woman than of Eve. Who would be able to sell her anything?

But enter the Serpent, and Eve has met her match. This silver-tongued con man points to the one thing she does not have: "the fruit of the tree that is in the midst of the garden."

This is Satan's well-honed skill—to lure us into wanting things that are forbidden. Satan whispers, "She's beautiful, and you should have her. Your life will be so much more exciting." And a married man is lured into sleeping with his secretary. A teenager knows that getting high is harmful, but the acceptance of the "cooler" kids is irresistible. The Devil quietly suggests, "Hey, no harm no foul. These guys are the ones to hang with. What's a little taste?" Never mind that infidelity with Sarah the Secretary will lead to the destruction of the man's marriage and the devastation of his wife and three young children. And sure, Pothead Pete and the gang will one day take it too far and flip their hemp-infested van on the interstate. But Satan makes adultery and drugs look so pleasurable that *not having them* is just too much to bear.

So even though God says that "the day that you eat of it you shall surely die," Eve, and then Adam, eat the forbidden fruit. Why? Because they "saw that the tree was good for food, and that it was a delight to the eyes." The fruit was spiritual poison, sentencing the human race to condemnation, but Satan sure did make it look sweet and tasty.

How do we fight Satan's bark of pleasure? We simply say, "Satan, you're wrong again! I see several more moves ahead than you want me to see. You want me to be blinded by the glitter and shine—the pleasure of the moment. Yet with the eyes of faith I can see that this dishonors my Savior and will eventually do me and those I love great harm." God has given us His Word and His Spirit to allow us a deeper glimpse into reality. As the psalmist says, "In your light do we see light" (Psalm 36:9). We know that Satan's promise of pleasure is momentary at best and always leaves a bitter aftertaste.

Consider Moses, who would not be duped by the siren-like promises of sin and boldly rejected the Devil's promises. "By faith Moses, when he was grown up, refused to be called the son of Pharaoh's daughter, choosing rather to be mistreated with the people of God than to enjoy the fleeting pleasures of sin" (Hebrews 11:24–25). Moses was confronted with the same choice that confronts us: the Devil's promises or God's promises. It really is that simple.

John Piper agrees: "No one sins out of duty. We sin because we believe the deceitful promises sin makes . . . Battling unbelief . . . means that we fight fire with fire. We throw against the promises of sin the promises of God. We take hold of some great promise God made about our future and say to a particular sin, 'Match that!'"[3]

Satan may keep on barking at us, telling us how liberating, how pleasurable his promises are. But let's not be fooled. Let's tell him we see through the smoke and mirrors of his lies. The promises of God are our pleasure and treasure.

---

3. John Piper, *Battling Unbelief* (Sisters, OR: Multnomah, 2007), 20.

BARK #3: SELF-JUSTIFICATION

Satan's third bark and most subtle tactic is the whisper of self-justification. This is the opposite of guilt, but it is equally damaging. Satan brings this attack through phrases like "It really wasn't that bad—many do far worse," or "Don't be so hard on yourself—she certainly did provoke you when you were just minding your own business," or "You had a right to chew him out—he's been a jerk to you all the time." Once these ideas take root in the mind, they are almost impossible to eradicate.

In essence, Satan persuades us that our need for Christ is not as great as we think. Remember, Satan hates the glory and beauty of Jesus, and he considers any diminishing of Christ a great victory. Rather than looking to our Savior and His righteousness, we are lulled into believing that we have a little bit of our own righteousness to add to the mix. After all, we aren't "that bad," right?

When we succumb to this temptation, we go wrong on two major fronts: we soften sin and we lessen grace.

For instance, men who say, "It was only a *little bit* of pornography" defy God's holiness and redefine God's moral law. What an audacious and wicked thing to do. Women who think, "I only trashed my husband a *little bit* to my friends," are really saying that they do not need Christ's cleansing blood as much as the criminals featured on the eleven o'clock news. So subtle is this kind of thinking that many never realize they have become the Pharisee in Jesus' parable.

> "Two men went up into the temple to pray, one a Pharisee and the other a tax collector. The Pharisee, standing by himself, prayed thus: 'God, I thank you that I am not like other men, extortioners, unjust, adulterers, or even like this tax collector. I fast twice a week; I give tithes of all that I get.'" (Luke 18:10–12)

The moment we buy into the lie of our "little bit of sinfulness," we see ourselves as better than others and less in need of God's grace. "Beware of self-righteousness," said Spurgeon. "The black devil of licentiousness destroys his hundreds, but the white devil of self-righteousness destroys his thousands."[4]

Combating Satan's bark of self-justification really comes down to one thing: humility. The moment we stop thinking of ourselves as sinners in need of a Savior is the moment of our defeat. The wisest, godliest people are always those most aware of their own sin.

John Newton, the author of "Amazing Grace," had much about which he could have boasted. He was a gifted hymn writer, minister, and theologian. So influential was his ministry in the life of William Wilberforce, the statesman who almost singlehandedly abolished slavery in Great Britain, that many see Newton as the spiritual force behind England's most significant social transformation in its history. Interestingly, as John Newton aged, he often remarked that there were only two things he wished to remember: "I am a great sinner, and Christ is a great Savior."

In his humility, Newton becomes a model for us. Our spiritual accomplishments do nothing to negate "the little bit of sin" that is in our lives. Our hope is only in Jesus, and "but for the grace of God, there go I."

So we learn to deafen our ears to the seductive whisper that we really aren't "that bad." And we face the Devil down with our response: No, Satan, you are wrong! I am that bad, but Christ is that much better. I will not trivialize my sin like you want me to. So ugly was my sin that Jesus needed to agonize and die to forgive it. So take your self-justification and hit the road, Satan. I will take my stand on the righteousness of Jesus himself.

---

4. From the sermon "Salvation All of Grace."

NO NEED TO BE POLITE

One of the most crucial skills of a good teacher is to be polite and patient when confronted by a stupid question or a goofy idea. As a pastor, I must remember this all the time. I have heard some things so inane that I want to shout, "You are so wrong!" Yet pastors who treat people like this won't last long—nor should they. Instead, I must bite my tongue and say those dreaded words, "Hmm . . . I can appreciate your perspective on that." Tongue-biting can be a very painful experience!

This is one of the reasons learning to tell Satan that he is wrong has been so refreshing for me. I rarely get to be this blunt with anyone. So when Satan comes with his bill of goods: "You're guilty" or "You deserve this break" or "Aww . . . you're really not that bad," I love to shout, "Satan, you are wrong!"

I invite you to do the same. There is no need to be polite with the enemy of our souls.

QUESTIONS FOR REFLECTION

1. What do you think of the old saying, "Sticks and stones may break my bones, but words will never hurt me"? Can you think of an example from childhood where words did far more damage to you than sticks or stones?
2. Read Proverbs 15:1, 18:21, and James 3:5. In light of these verses, why do you think Satan puts so much effort into words?
3. Can you think of other "barks" besides guilt, pleasure, and self-justification? If so, give some examples. How would you suggest fighting them?
4. Read Luke 18:10–12. How would you use this passage to help someone detect and then fight the temptation of self-justification?
5. What is a "bark" that you need to battle in your life right now? What specific steps do you take to silence Satan's bark?

I'm not afraid of death; I just don't want to be there
when it happens.

—WOODY ALLEN

Hopeless subjection to death characterizes earthly
existence apart from the intervention of God.

—WILLIAM LANE CRAIG

O death, where is your victory? O death, where is
your sting?

—1 CORINTHIANS 15:55

CHAPTER NINE

SATAN, YOU DON'T SCARE ME!

The only thing we have to fear is fear itself."

"Fear knocked at the door. Faith answered. And lo, no one was there."

"I will show you fear in a handful of dust."[1]

There are many famous quotes about fear, most promising some kind of vague power to rise above it or ignore it altogether. They look good encased in decorative frames and hung on our walls, but they are of little help when we stare death in the face. Somehow clever clichés don't seem to be enough to ease our dread when the moment of truth comes.

A man crosses the street and suddenly faces the fast-approaching car that will end his life. A woman discovers a deranged serial killer in her apartment. A young person gets a diagnosis of incurable cancer. Does anyone think that Hallmark-like sentiments about conquering fear would even remotely help in any of these situations? Let's face it, at the root of all our fears lurks the ultimate fear: the fear of death.

---

1. From (1) Franklin Delano Roosevelt, First Inaugural Address; (2) Author Unknown; (3) T. S. Eliot, "The Waste Land."

THE BIBLE DOES NOT SUGARCOAT THE FEAR OF DEATH

It is common in our culture to speak of death as *natural*. Whether it is the biologist claiming that death is as natural as birth, or a cast of Disney characters singing about the "Circle of Life," death is usually given either the sentimental or the velvet-touch treatment. Not so in the Bible. God's Word is unflinching: death is anything but natural—it is the enemy.

Death is anything but natural—it is the enemy.

I remember in a college English class reading Dylan Thomas's famous poem "Do Not Go Gentle into That Good Night." Thomas wrote this as an ode to his dying father, and it is haunting in its emotional tone. The refrain throughout the poem is "Do not go gentle into that good night. Rage, rage against the dying of the light." I will never forget the patronizing look on my professor's face as he reflected, "Poor Mr. Thomas. He does not want his father to die. There is something tragic about a man who cannot come to terms with the natural cycle of life." Many of my peers nodded in that smugly self-satisfied way of "enlightened" students who have risen above the less fortunate peons in society who lack their collegiate wisdom. I had only been a Christian for a couple of years at that point, and while I wasn't sure why, something seemed off about this perspective. Only later did I learn that the Bible agreed with Dylan Thomas—not my professor.

One is hard-pressed to find support for the naturalness of death in the Bible. Instead, there is much to suggest that death is anything but natural. Consider some of the following passages.

> "If, because of one man's trespass, *death reigned* through that one man. . . ." (Romans 5:17)

> "The *last enemy* to be destroyed is death." (1 Corinthians 15:26)

"He is torn from the tent in which he trusted and is brought to the *king of terrors*." (Job 18:14)

Do you realize that death has just been personified as a ruthless dictator, an enemy, and the ultimate terrorist? Does that sound *natural* to you?

In the clearest passage on the subject of death's origin, the apostle Paul writes,

Therefore, just as sin came into the world through one man, and *death through sin*, and so death spread to all men because all sinned. . . ." (Romans 5:12)

Death gained entrance into the world through sin. And sin is, as theologian Neal Plantinga has summarized, "not the way it's supposed to be."[2] The world God created was perfect. Sin broke into God's paradise and destroyed that perfect harmony. Death piggybacked on sin, and ever since, the world has known sickness, despair, and pain. Death is not natural!

Dylan Thomas expressed an ancient sentiment. We were not meant to die, and deep down, one way or another, we fight against it with all our might, even if it's by denial. We do, indeed, rage against the dying of the light. In our heart of hearts we know that death is cruel, and we fear it. And Satan knows we fear it.

WHAT SATAN DOES WITH OUR FEAR OF DEATH

I hate torture scenes in movies or television shows. I cannot bear to watch someone being tormented—even when I know it's an actor and it's not real. Even as I try to think of an example, I

---

2. See Cornelius Plantinga, *Not the Way It's Supposed to Be: A Breviary of Sin* (Grand Rapids: Eerdmans, 1995).

cringe! I don't even want to write about it. But Satan, the ultimate tormentor, doesn't cringe. He doesn't blink. Like a villain pressing down on the hero's open wound, Satan loves to press down on our fear of death. He exploits the opportunity presented by our own dread.

Human beings are "those who all their lives were held in slavery by their fear of death," and they must toil under the power of "him who holds the power of death—that is, the devil" (Hebrews 2:14-15 NIV). The implications of this picture are profound. Every human life, no matter how happy and rich with meaning, is lived under a dark and foreboding cloud. We joke about "death and taxes" as life's only certainties, but if we were honest, we would take a whole year of April fifteenths over the alternative, wouldn't we? This is why we rarely think about death, and the few times we are forced to, we retreat into denial at the first opportunity. The Bible has a name for this kind of subterranean fear—always just below the surface of our conscious lives—slavery.

Satan is happy to throw out multiple distractions to keep people from ever even considering what lies beyond the grave.

"Those who all their lives were held in slavery by their fear of death," are very easy to manipulate. People who don't want to face their fear of death will happily immerse themselves in work, family, hobbies, entertainment, drugs, sex, or sports to insure that their minds never have to linger on the what-happens-when-it's-all-over question. All the while Satan is happy to throw out multiple distractions to keep people from ever even considering what lies beyond the grave. And what happens when we do find our minds drawn to our own mortality? The Devil is right there to whip up our fear. "What if it is just total unending darkness?" "What if it is worse than darkness?" "This life which you have enjoyed is over.

No more family vacations, no more mornings at Starbucks! It's all done." This is the kind of fear our enemy relishes. Not the silly kind of Hollywood-horror fear we considered earlier, but the deep, abiding fear of the grave that hangs around our neck like an albatross. Well, it used to anyway.

HOW JESUS' DEATH PREPARES US FOR OUR OWN

While we have considered a couple phrases from Hebrews 2, we have yet to look at the big picture. And we need to do that, because in just two verses, the writer of Hebrews explains why the great burden of fearful people facing their own deaths evaporates like water in a kettle.

> Since the children have flesh and blood, he too shared in their humanity so that by his death he might destroy him who holds the power of death—that is, the devil—and free those who all their lives were held in slavery by their fear of death. (Hebrews 2:14–15 NIV)

Earlier we considered how Jesus' death brings about our complete acquittal before God: there is now no condemnation for the Christian. Here, the book of Hebrews shows another wonderful effect of the cross. Jesus' sacrifice was also able to "destroy him who holds the power of death—that is, the devil." In order to celebrate this victory though, we must first know exactly what kind of power Satan had.

Satan has the power *of* death, not the power *over* death. Scripture is clear: God, and God alone, has the power over life and death. He, not the Devil, decides when a person is born and when a person dies. King David testifies to this truth when

Satan has the power *of* death, not the power *over* death.

he says, "Your eyes saw my unformed substance; in your book were written, every one of them, the days that were formed for me, when as yet there was none of them" (Psalm 139:16). The book of each person's life, from birth to death, belongs to God, not Satan. So Satan's power in death is something other than control (even though we can be sure he would love to have it).

The text that gives us the clearest clue to Satan's power in death comes from the apostle Paul's pen: "The sting of death is sin, and the power of sin is the law" (1 Corinthians 15:56). What makes death so dreadful is sin. But why? Because what gives sin its "sting" is the law. What Paul is telling us is crucial in understanding Satan's power in death. Follow Paul's logic.

> Step 1: People die, but what makes that so horrible is that they die as sinners.
>
> Step 2: Dying as sinners is bad, but what makes that so horrible is that they die as law-breakers—not just any old law, but God's law.

We now ask the most important question: What is so bad about dying as one who has broken God's law? The answer is simple but devastating: We enter eternity unprepared to meet a holy and righteous God and are consigned to eternal separation from Him.

Ultimately, people fear death because at some level they know they are not prepared to stand before God because their sin has never been properly dealt with. This is why Paul says, "The sting of death is sin."

Satan's aim is to keep sinners in this unprepared state so that when they die, they are doomed. John Piper says it well.

> The only weapon the devil can use to destroy us in death is our sin. Nobody goes to hell because they are oppressed by the devil or even possessed by the devil. Nobody goes to hell because they are harassed by the devil

or get shot at by the devil or are given hallucinations by the devil. These are all smoke screens to hide the one deadly power in Satan's artillery, namely, unforgiven sin. The only reason anybody goes to hell is because of his own sin. And all Satan can do is fight like hell to keep you sinning and to keep you away from the one who forgives sin.[3]

Now we can appreciate why the Christian can say, "Satan, you don't scare me."

By dying for sinners, Jesus has taken away our lack of preparedness for eternity. Our sin has been forgiven; we have been acquitted; and we are now ready to stand before God at the very moment of our death. This is why the apostle Paul can ask, "O death, where is your victory? O death, where is your sting?" (1 Corinthians 15:55). Christians are now forever freed from what once held them in an unyielding grip. The fear of death has now been replaced with the assurance of life—in this world and in the glorious life after death.

REALISM FOR THOSE FACING DEATH

I must close this chapter with a word of caution, however. We must beware of overreaching in our desire to find assurance in Christ's victory over Satan and death. Years ago I talked to a woman who was weeks away from death. She was a strong believer in Christ. She had served Him for years. She was an example to many of how to live full-out for the glory of God. Needless to say, then, I was surprised when she asked me to meet her to confess a terrible sin. Sitting in her hospital room, I listened to her simple and direct confession. "I am ashamed to admit it, but I am terribly afraid."

How would I counsel her? Should I direct her confession Godward and tell her to bask in the forgiveness she had in Jesus? After

---

3. http://www.soundofgrace.com/piper96/06-23-96.htm

all, she knew Hebrews 2:14–15 and its glorious pronouncement that there was no more reason to fear death. Why couldn't this woman face death bravely? Yet as we talked, it became clear to me that she did not fear death; she feared dying.

There is a big difference between *death* as a final destination and *dying* as a prolonged process that gets us there. This dear woman was concerned about very real and legitimate questions—the same questions most, if not all, of us would have. What would dying feel like? How much would it hurt? What would she feel in those final moments? What Jesus has solved is our destination problem. The other side of the grave is a safe place—more than safe; it is glorious! We can have full assurance that there is nothing to fear on the other side. Those who know Jesus as Savior can rest in these truths. But the act of dying is understandably fearful, and we who are not yet facing it need to be sensitive, pastoral, and patient with people's fears.

> There is a big difference between *death* as a final destination and *dying* as a prolonged process that gets us there.

So if you or someone you love is facing the nearness of death, may I urge you to celebrate the great destiny Jesus has secured for us? If you or someone close to you is struggling with the act of dying, then I hope you will surround yourself or the one suffering with people who will sensitively and lovingly be with you throughout the process. The apprehension over the process of dying is understandable, but what a comfort to know that Jesus is waiting on the other side.

The first question and answer in the Heidelberg Catechism is one of the most beautiful things ever written. It comforts in life and death.

Question 1: What is thy only comfort in life and death?

That I with body and soul, both in life and death, am not my own, but belong unto my faithful Saviour Jesus Christ, who, with His precious blood, has fully satisfied for all my sins, and delivered me from all the power of the devil; and so preserves me that without the will of my heavenly Father not a hair can fall from my head; yea, that all things must be subservient to my salvation, and therefore, by His Holy Spirit, He also assures me of eternal life, and makes me heartily willing and ready, henceforth, to live unto Him.

QUESTIONS FOR REFLECTION

1. Did you grow up thinking that death was simply a natural part of life? Can you think of examples in our culture that promote this view of death?

2. Read Romans 5:17, 1 Corinthians 15:26, and Job 18:14. Based on these passages, write a short description of the Bible's portrait of death. How does this picture differ from the one painted by our culture?

3. Read Hebrews 2:14–15. Imagine that you are talking to a non-Christian friend who is admitting that he hates even thinking about death. How might you use this verse to tell him that the Bible understands this desire to avoid the subject of death?

4. Read 1 Corinthians 15:55–56. How would you paraphrase this passage in a way that might be more understandable to an unbeliever?

You're fired!

—DONALD TRUMP

Satan doth not tempt God's children because they have sin in them, but because they have grace in them. Had they no grace, the devil would not disturb them. Though to be tempted is a trouble, yet to think why you are tempted is a comfort.

—THOMAS BROOKS

For the grace of God that brings salvation has appeared to all men. It teaches us to say "No" to ungodliness and worldly passions, and to live self-controlled, upright and godly lives in this present age.

—TITUS 2:11-12 (NIV)

CHAPTER TEN

SATAN, YOU'RE FIRED!

It is amazing what you can find on the Internet these days. Do a search sometime on the phrase "fire your boss." Countless Web sites pop up, covering every possible aspect of the topic—everything from starting your own business to filing the proper paperwork with your HR department to getting your supervisor canned. Obviously there is quite a market for those who dream about getting out from under the oppressive reign of a difficult boss. Yet it seems most people just accept unbearable managers as an inevitable (and usually unalterable) fact of life. So we buckle down, keep our heads low, do our work well, and try to keep our contact with the boss to a bare minimum.

Interestingly, we find a similar picture of humanity in the second chapter of Ephesians.

> And you were dead in the trespasses and sins in which you
> once walked, following the course of this world, following the
> prince of the power of the air, the spirit that is now at work in
> the sons of disobedience—among whom we all once lived in
> the passions of our flesh, carrying out the desires of the body
> and the mind, and were by nature children of wrath, like the
> rest of mankind. (Ephesians 2:1–3)

Here is the classic picture of people outside of the redeeming work of God. They are busy at work "carrying out the desires of the body and the mind," but they are doing this under the supervision of their boss, "the prince of the power of the air."[1] Apparently Satan is such an effective administrator that his employees carry out his agenda quite successfully: "the spirit that is now at work in the sons of disobedience." Yet *boss* is really too soft a word; in reality, the Devil is a slave driver. Sadly there is even less hope of firing a slave driver than a boss.

Of course by this point, you already know that Jesus has fired him for us!

A GREAT JOB TRANSFER

The Bible has a number of ways to express the radical change that takes place when a sinner becomes a saint. One of those ways is to describe it as a relocation from one place to another. Think of it as the world's best job transfer.

He drew me up *from the pit of destruction*, out of the miry bog, and *set my feet upon a rock*, making my steps secure. (Psalm 40:2)

He has delivered us *from the domain of darkness* and transferred us to the kingdom of his beloved Son, in whom we have redemption, the forgiveness of sins. (Colossians 1:13–14)

---

1. Many teachers have ventured a number of educated guesses on the exact meaning of this unusual title for Satan. I prefer F. F. Bruce's more simple approach when he writes, "Paul was not necessarily accepting the current notion of the air being the abode and realm of evil spirits. Basically his thought was of an evil power with control in the world, but whose existence was not material but spiritual." F. F. Bruce, *Ephesians* TNTC (Grand Rapids: Eerdmans, 1989).

But you are a chosen race, a royal priesthood, a holy nation, a people for his own possession, that you may proclaim the excellencies of him who called you *out of darkness into his marvelous light*. (1 Peter 2:9)

The Christian lives in a new environment. Yes, we still inhabit the same body and live at the same address, but in the spiritual realm we stand on God's turf. No matter how much Satan may want to keep us on his census rolls, we have citizenship in another town. "Our citizenship is in heaven, and from it we await a Savior, the Lord Jesus Christ" (Philippians 3:20). We are living free in enemy territory!

We are living free in enemy territory!

As good as this new "workplace" is, however, we would still be living in misery if we kept the same boss. The good news is that not only do believers have a new workplace; we also have a new boss. A change in location is just window dressing unless the inhabitants have changed as well. Jesus did not simply die to give us a new realm of existence, but a new master as well.

FROM SATAN TO GOD, FROM SIN TO RIGHTEOUSNESS

How would a man who had once hated Christ, persecuted Christians, and crusaded to rid the world of even the faintest traces of the church communicate his 180-degree change of heart? This was the unique challenge of the man once known as Saul of Tarsus, who would become the apostle Paul, the great champion for Christ, the gospel, and the church. He had several avenues of explanation available to him.

He could have used the educational rationale. As an educated man, he could have claimed that his great learning had sent him on an academic quest to assess this new Christian faith on historical or philosophical grounds. After thorough research, he realized that the historical biography of Jesus of Nazareth matched the prophetic profile of the Messiah in the Old Testament, which it certainly did. Yet Paul never attributed his conversion to his own intellectual investigation.

Or he could have chosen the sociological path as plausible grounds for his radical transformation. After spending time among Christians, he was drawn to the way they interacted, loved, and served one another. Such wonderful fellowship was not his experience in the judgmental world of Pharisaic Judaism, and the acceptance he felt among Christians made him a true believer. However, while Paul certainly would come to love the unique kind of life within the Christian community, he never once suggested that his conversion was based on it.

Interestingly, the best window into Paul's turnaround-tale is found in his own understanding of what God wanted him to do with the rest of his life. On one occasion Paul shared his testimony with King Agrippa, a powerful man who was more than curious about this man Paul, who was being brought before the Roman authorities by "the chief priests and the principal men of the Jews," who were "bringing many and serious charges against him that they could not prove" (Acts 25:2, 7).

"I would like to hear the man myself," Agrippa said (Acts 25:22). So Paul shared his story of the blinding light and the voice from heaven that stopped him dead in his tracks. Then he launched right into the mission God had given him to fulfill: to preach the message of Christ among lost people, "to open their eyes, so that they may *turn from darkness to light* and *from the power of Satan to God,* that they may receive forgiveness of sins" (Acts 26:18). Paul understood that becoming a Christian was ultimately about being released from the domination of the cruel taskmaster Satan and handed over to the loving care of God himself. In other words, Satan had old Saul of Tarsus in a death grip, but Christ set him free to be the servant of the only worthy master, God himself. Author Sam Storms vividly captures this kind of exchange when he writes that God has "extricated us from the grip of Satan and now embraces us with an eternal and irrevocable love."[2]

> Paul saw the entire Christian life as an opportunity to please and serve a new master.

It should not surprise us then that Paul saw the entire Christian life as an opportunity to please and serve a new master. In one small section of the book of Romans, he highlights this theme several times.

> But thanks be to God, that you who were *once slaves of sin* have become obedient from the heart to the standard of teaching to which you were committed, and, having been set free from sin, *have become slaves of righteousness.* (Romans 6:17–18)

> For just as you once presented your members as *slaves to impurity and to lawlessness* leading to more lawlessness, so *now* present your members as *slaves to righteousness* leading to sanctification. (Romans 6:19)

> But now . . . you have been *set free from sin* and *have become slaves of God.* (Romans 6:22)

It is interesting that the act of being set free from sin did not lead to some kind of do-your-own-thing individual freedom. Paul

---

2. Sam Storms, *The Hope of Glory: 100 Daily Meditations on Colossians* (Wheaton, IL: Crossway, 2007).

understands that people always have a master; they always serve something or someone. As Charles Spurgeon observed:

> There is no in-between—there does not appear to be a moment left for an independent state, but out of one servitude we pass into another . . . As we were governed and swayed by the love of sin, so we become, in a similar manner, subject to the forces of Grace and the Truth of God! As sin took possession of us and controlled our acts, so Grace claims us as its own, takes possession of us and rules us with an absolute sway.[3]

In no sense whatsoever does Satan have any hold or claim over the life of the believer.

In no sense whatsoever does Satan have any hold or claim over the life of the believer. The Christian belongs to Jesus Christ and needs to take his marching orders from Christ alone.

SATAN STILL BARKS LIKE HE OWNS US

The implications of our new status as God's servants are striking. We are not obliged to do one thing Satan wants us to. Before Jesus saved us, we were entirely under the Devil's sway. He ordered, and we marched. He tempted, and we succumbed. He said, "jump," and we happily inquired about the desired height. Now we are free from his cruel tyranny, even though he does not want us to think so.

Satan is the classic schoolyard bully, taunting, promising, tempting, and threatening us. The schoolyard does not belong to him though. While the Devil barks, God simply stands beside us saying, "He cannot harm you. He is not in charge. I am."

Of course, we can *choose* to act like Satan is still in charge; we

---

3. C. H. Spurgeon, "Our Change of Masters," http://www.spurgeongems.org/vols25-27/chs1482.pdf, accessed on 1/28/11.

do it all the time. But what could be more tragic than that we, who have been set free from our former slave master, go crawling back to him like he owns us? Like P. T. Barnum, our enemy must smile as he thinks, "There truly is a sucker born every minute."

Whenever we live for ourselves, for our lusts and passions, we are playing right into Satan's hands. Remember, this is how we were described *before* coming to know Christ: "We all once lived in the passions of our flesh, carrying out the desires of the body and the mind" (Ephesians 2:3). The unbelieving world has no choice but to live like this. Its citizenship is right here in the "world," where Satan is given his temporary license to rule and wreak havoc. Yet for those who have been set free from the Devil's reign, "the grace of God that brings salvation has appeared to all men. It teaches us to say 'No' to ungodliness and worldly passions, and to live self-controlled, upright and godly lives in this present age" (Titus 2:11–12 NIV). And because we swear ultimate allegiance to a new master, King Jesus, we can boldly say, "Satan, you're fired!" We owe him absolutely nothing, have already given him too much, and we now want to spend the rest of our lives pleasing our new king.

> Because we swear ultimate allegiance to a new master, King Jesus, we can boldly say, "Satan, you're fired!"

MASTERING NEW ROUTES

I have a church office, but my congregation knows they have a better chance of running into me at the local Starbucks, my true office. It is my habit to drive there almost every weekday morning. A few weeks ago, I had a physical scheduled for eight o'clock in the morning. Knowing it was out of my routine, I put the appointment in my smart phone, wrote it on the kitchen calendar, and asked my wife to remind me that morning. All three safeguards worked, and I got in my car and headed for my doctor's office with five minutes to spare. Ten minutes later I pulled into my usual parking spot at Starbucks! Good thing I had that five-minute cushion; I ended up being only ten minutes late for my appointment!

It is hard to get out of ruts and start traveling new routes, isn't it? I go to that coffee oasis so much that my car seems to transport me there by autopilot. The same holds true in spiritual things. Most people develop such ruts when living outside of a saving relationship with Christ that learning to take new routes just seems counter-intuitive. A man who spent every night looking at pornography can hardly imagine a night without it. The teenager who spent every waking minute on Facebook, suffering the loss of grades (and actual human friendships), initially feels like she's trapped on a desert island when she goes a whole hour not updating her status. The gossip-loving employee wonders how he will get through a single workday without assassinating a co-worker. Worst of all, our old slave driver keeps barking, "Do it! Scratch that itch! Stop being such a stick-in-the-mud!" It's so natural to fall back into the old rut. Yet such times of temptation are opportunities for victory.

Consider the example Paul uses, writing of marriage. "Be angry and do not sin; do not let the sun go down on your anger, and give no opportunity to the devil" (Ephesians 4:26–27). Here we have a husband who *knows* he is right, and a wife who *knows* she is right. What started as a mild disagreement has escalated in a hurry. The man is thinking, "I'll grab my pillow, slam the door shut, and crash on the sofa. I'm not putting up with this anymore." She is thinking, "I should just say it. I never should have married you! You have made me the unhappiest wife in the world." All the while, Satan is rooting, "Do it! Say it! Let's get this party started!" Those without Christ, the gospel, the indwelling power of the Spirit, and the example of other Christian couples who have endured don't stand a chance. But those who have these blessings can actually make a choice. "No, Satan!

You're fired! You don't own me anymore. I belong to a new Master, and He wants me to die to myself and put my partner first. I'm asking for His grace to empower me right now!"

Sadly even we who are believers fall back into those familiar ruts. And what is the result? We give an *opportunity to the Devil*. Satan exploits the moment of weakness, and next time it is even easier to push the couple toward uglier, nastier fights. And maybe, just maybe, if all goes well, the couple will end up before a judge working out custody arrangements.

How woefully sad when Christians allow Satan to assert himself as boss again. He has no right to it, so why even give him an inch? We need to pray like the old Puritan who knew the need for watchfulness and strength to resist the enemy of our souls.

QUESTIONS FOR REFLECTION

1. Have you ever wished that you could fire your boss? Why do you think so many people wish they could fire their boss?
2. Read Ephesians 2:1–4. In what sense is Satan the "boss" of people outside of Christ?
3. Read Romans 6:17–22. Note the specific references to leaving one kind of slavery to come under another. Think back on your Christian experience. Can you remember moments when the lordship of Jesus transformed a particular area in your life?
4. Read Titus 2:11–12. What role does God's grace have in dealing with ungodliness? Is this normally the way we think of God's grace?
5. Can you think of areas in your life where you need to "fire" Satan?

I have found out there ain't no surer way to find out whether you like people or hate them than to travel with them.

—MARK TWAIN

Since Christ is thus comfortably set out to us, let us not believe Satan's representations of him. When we are troubled in conscience for our sins, Satan's manner is then to present Christ to the afflicted soul as a most severe judge armed with justice against us. But then let us present him to our souls as offered to our view by God himself, holding out a scepter of mercy, and spreading his arms to receive us.

—RICHARD SIBBES

Let love be genuine. Abhor what is evil; hold fast to what is good.

—ROMANS 12:9

CHAPTER ELEVEN

SATAN, YOU DISGUST ME!

Titles are tricky. They are intended to hook people and make them want to discover more. Yet due to their brevity, sometimes titles leave a powerful misimpression. I once preached a sermon called "Just Sit Down and Shut Up." Let me give a friendly piece of advice to any aspiring preachers out there. Don't do this! I had every hope that my message on "letting God speak to you through His word" would be greatly aided by such a clever title. The only thing it aided me in, however, was responding to e-mails about why I would choose such a crass and shocking sermon title. In a similar way, the title of this chapter, "Satan, You Disgust Me!" could backfire if it leaves the impression of a spiritualized "You're a Mean One, Mr. Grinch." That song is a classic. My kids and I love the line, "You nauseate me, Mr. Grinch! With a nauseous super naus!" Our Christmas is just not complete until we have sung a few bars of some of the best character assassination ever penned. Mockery of this kind is fictional fun, just a little bit of silly talk for the sake of humor. But when I invite you to say, "Satan, you disgust me!" my intention is anything but silly.

Sometimes the only way to appreciate something is to contrast it with something inferior. We tell our children to compare their current violin playing to the dying-like-drowning-cats sound they were producing just six months earlier. The woman who gets a first-class makeover looks at her "before" shot to appreciate the improvement in her appearance. Detergent commercials proudly show off white T-shirts that gleam like freshly fallen snow next to the lackluster faded white shirts of those cleaned with "other leading brands." Sometimes we need to look at something ugly or less attractive to better appreciate something lovely.

A TALE OF TWO KINGS

Matthew seems to have had this comparison/contrast method in mind when he recorded the events surrounding Christ's birth. By referencing the visit of the Magi, it is obvious that he wants the reader to appreciate and adore the baby born in Bethlehem. If these mysterious visitors from the East (who, by the way, were not even Jewish) were willing to make such a long and dangerous journey, then how glorious must this Child be? And how much more should *we* worship and adore Him, knowing what He was born to do for us? Of course, Matthew includes more by way of contrast than the story of the Magi. He also tells a story of two kings, and by pondering the vile nature of the one, we will better appreciate the excellent nature of the other.

> Now after Jesus was born in Bethlehem of Judea in the days of Herod the king, behold, wise men from the east came to Jerusalem, saying, "Where is he who has been born king of the Jews? For we saw his star when it rose and have come to worship him." (Matthew 2:1–2)

In just two verses, Matthew invites us to contrast the two kings. Perhaps the Magi never realized the ironic nature of their question to King Herod. They were asking the king (small k) where the King (capital K) was residing. And Herod did not like the implications of this question one bit. So let's consider the stark differences between these two kings—between Herod, the wannabe king, and Jesus, the true king.

The wannabe king scrambles to protect his kingship; the true king entrusts His kingship to His Father. Unlike the Magi who were overjoyed at the thought of the Messiah's arrival, "When Herod the king heard this, he was troubled, and all Jerusalem with him" (Matthew 2:3). The wannabe king is threatened by the arrival of another king, and he is shaken to the core. Jerusalem is troubled, no doubt, because when Herod isn't happy, nobody's happy.

Immediately Herod goes into emergency management mode and slickly ascertains the whereabouts of this infant threat. "Then Herod summoned the wise men secretly and ascertained from them what time the star had appeared. And he sent them to Bethlehem, saying, 'Go and search diligently for the child, and when you have found him, bring me word, that I too may come and worship him'" (Matthew 2:7–8). Once he discovers the child's whereabouts, of course, Herod can do what he really wants to, and it has nothing to do with worship.

Now contrast Jesus with this wannabe king. The true king does not scramble to hold onto what is rightfully His. Though He was worshipped in eternity by countless angels, and though the universe exists to do His bidding,[1] Jesus left His throne of power and came into our world as a helpless baby.[2] He was not under the protection

---

1. "And again, when he brings the firstborn into the world, he says, 'Let all God's angels worship him'" (Hebrews 1:6). "For by him all things were created, in heaven and on earth, visible and invisible, whether thrones or dominions or rulers or authorities—all things were created through him and for him" (Colossians 1:16).

2. "Though he was in the form of God, [he] did not count equality with God a thing to be grasped, but made himself nothing, taking the form of a servant, being born in the likeness of men" (Philippians 2:6–7).

of angels or armed guards but of a nervous young couple who were almost swallowed up in the epic drama. In pondering such an amazing truth, Martin Luther said, "The mystery of Christ, that He sunk Himself into our flesh, is beyond all human understanding." This is a humble king, a monarch willing to put himself in the most vulnerable of positions for a greater good. What a marvelous king! And we see His glory more clearly against the backdrop of Herod's insecurity.

The true king saves His own subjects at immense personal cost; the wannabe king will kill his own subjects for his own gain.

The true king saves His own subjects at immense personal cost; the wannabe king will kill his own subjects for his own gain. Herod orders his soldiers to do the unthinkable: "Then Herod, when he saw that he had been tricked by the wise men, became furious, and he sent and killed all the male children in Bethlehem and in all that region who were two years old or under, according to the time that he had ascertained from the wise men" (Matthew 2:16). So loathsome and detestable is Herod that he slaughters scores of innocent children. As king it is his duty to protect his subjects, particularly the most defenseless of his subjects. Yet Herod cares only about one thing: Herod. All wannabe kings do.

Just a few verses before recording Herod's massacre, Matthew sets up another contrast. The angel has told Joseph that Mary will bear a miraculously conceived son, and that this baby has already been assigned a name by God the Father: "She will bear a son, and you shall call his name Jesus, for he will save his people from their sins" (Matthew 1:21). The name Jesus is a variant of Joshua, a wonderful Hebrew word which means, in essence, "God saves." The baby Messiah will bear this name to underscore His own mission: to *save His people from their sins*. There is a cross in this baby's future, and one day He will be nailed to it, agonize on it, and finally die on it for the sake of His subjects. Contrasting this with Herod's malevolence, we can see Jesus' glory and grace even more clearly. So we look at Herod, not out of some kind of morbid fascination, but to appreciate afresh the supreme, incomparable beauty of Jesus.

In the same way, when we look at Satan in all his ugliness, we bring the splendor of the Savior into greater focus.

Let's return to the verse we started with in chapter one: "The thief comes only to steal and kill and destroy. I came that they may have life and have it abundantly" (John 10:10). The contrast is clear: The thief versus Jesus. The life-taker versus the Life-Giver. The Savior wants His audience to note the difference, because in doing so, they will understand why He is to be desired above everything else.

NOT A TAKER, BUT A GIVER

Notice that *the thief comes only to steal*. He is a taker, through and through. This is so ironic since Satan presents himself as a giver. Think of the "promises" of freedom and contentment he made to Adam, Eve, and Jesus himself. He speaks as if he has a bag of endless goodies to offer, but in reality his sack is only to carry what he steals from us. Like the bully who goes out to steal other kids' Halloween candy, the Devil is on the prowl to fill his own bag with the treats of others.

In C. S. Lewis's classic book on demonic tactics, *The Screwtape Letters*, he puts some interesting words in the mouth of the seasoned tempter Uncle Screwtape as he advises his apprentice, Wormwood, on how to sabotage the Christian.

> Never forget that when we are dealing with any pleasure in its healthy and normal and satisfying form, we are, in a sense, on the Enemy's ground. I know we have won many a soul through pleasure. All the same, it is His invention, not ours. He made all the pleasures: all our research

so far has not enabled us to produce one. All we can do is to encourage the humans to take pleasures which our Enemy has produced, at times, or in ways, or in degrees, which He has forbidden.[3]

Lewis's observation is astute. Only God (the Enemy to the demonic realm) can create true pleasure and joy. Satan is not a creator but a manipulator. He has not one positive contribution to offer for any solitary life. How tragic that so many believe his bogus promises of peace, happiness, and fulfillment! All he can do is twist and pervert God's good gifts into something harmful.

Satan is not a creator but a manipulator. All he can do is twist and pervert God's good gifts into something harmful.

For example, Satan takes the beautiful gift of sex, something God designed for married couples to enjoy and strengthen their relationship for life, and turns it into a cheap thrill outside of marriage. He promises, "This will feel great, and you'll be a happier person for it." He conceals the fact that once the short-lived thrill is over, the emotional, physical, and spiritual pain will inevitably set in somewhere.

God provides us with food that is delicious and good for us physically, but Satan, acting like he invented it, promises satisfaction by eating "all you want, when you want." As people believe the lie, make food an idol, and live from one snack to the next, all Satan has done is robbed us of the good and healthy purpose of food. He is a thief, pure and simple.

Now consider Jesus. He is the supreme giver. When He meets a thirsty woman, He promises to give her water that will eternally slake her thirst. For blind Bartimaeus He offers sight. For wayward

---

3. C. S. Lewis, *The Screwtape Letters* (New York: HarperCollins, 2001), 44.

Mary Magdalene He provides grace and forgiveness. For the fearful He grants peace. For the confused He offers wisdom. For the weary He bestows rest. Read the Gospels and notice how often Jesus is giving of His time, His energy, and His very life.

In the context of John 10, the underlying contrast is between Satan (and the false teachers he inspires) as the thief and Jesus as the shepherd. How each deals with the sheep is significantly different. Commentator F. F. Bruce writes: "The thief's designs on the sheep are wholly malicious; the good shepherd's plans for them are entirely benevolent. He desires and promotes their wellbeing; he is not content that they should eke out a bare and miserable existence; he wants them to live life to the full, to have plenty of good pasturage and enjoy good health."[4]

NOT A SABOTEUR, BUT A SAVIOR

The thief also comes "to kill and destroy."[5] The thief wants to kill us spiritually, and Scripture's portrait of his life-stifling methods is clear. He snatches God's Word from hearts,[6] blinds eyes to the glory of Jesus,[7] lulls the unwary into a sense of false security,[8] and persuades us that other treasures are better than Christ.[9] The Devil

---

4. F. F. Bruce, *The Gospel of John* (Grand Rapids: Eerdmans, 1983), 226.

5. I am treating "kill and destroy" in the same category since both overflow from Satan's general desire to wreak havoc in the world.

6. "When anyone hears the word of the kingdom and does not understand it, the evil one comes and snatches away what has been sown in his heart. This is what was sown along the path" (Matthew 13:19).

7. "In their case the god of this world has blinded the minds of the unbelievers, to keep them from seeing the light of the gospel of the glory of Christ, who is the image of God" (2 Corinthians 4:4).

8. "And he came to the disciples and found them sleeping. And he said to Peter, 'So, could you not watch with me one hour? Watch and pray that you may not enter into temptation'" (Matthew 26:40–41).

9. "But I am afraid that as the serpent deceived Eve by his cunning, your thoughts will be led astray from a sincere and pure devotion to Christ" (2 Corinthians 11:3).

of Scripture must laugh at the silly portrayals of himself in pop culture. And all the while he is happy to kill and destroy in the ways that will bring people to eternal ruin. He is a master saboteur.

Think about that kind of evil for just a moment. An enemy who is consumed by the desire to end your earthly life is certainly evil. But an enemy who is obsessed with making sure that you are *eternally* damned, miserable every day without end—what kind of evil is that? J. I. Packer contemplates this level of malevolence with chilling precision:

> Scripture clearly means us to believe in a Satan, and a host of Satanic attendants, who are of quite unimaginable badness—more cruel, more malicious, more proud, more scornful, more perverted, more destructive, more disgusting, more filthy, more despicable, than anything our minds can conceive.[10]

We should have no hesitation saying, "Satan, you disgust me!"

Against the backdrop of such detestable villainy, Jesus emerges all the more wonderful, all the more captivating. "I came that they may have life and have it abundantly" (John 10:10).

How helpless we would be against the craftiness and power of our adversary without Jesus. Yet notice that Jesus is not merely a force who *lessens* the blow Satan unleashes on us; He completely *crushes* the Devil's plans and attacks. Remember, "The reason the Son of God appeared was *to destroy the works of the devil*" (1 John 3:8). Jesus does not merely counter Satan or neutralize him; He *destroys* him.

The Son of God tells the Devil: "I know you mean to bring this life to eternal ruin. But I will not let you. This one is Mine, and

---

10. http://www.matthiasmedia.com.au/briefing/library/2151, accessed January 21, 2011.

not only will I shield him from you, but I will see to it that he has life—and not just any kind of life, but abundant life."

By considering the depth of Satan's wickedness, we are able to magnify the name of Jesus even more. What a joy to think how much the Devil must hate that!

> Jesus is not merely a force who *lessens* the blow Satan unleashes on us; He completely *crushes* the Devil's plans and attacks.

MY BOY IN MY ARMS

At the beginning of this book, I told you about holding my young son in my arms after a particularly nasty dream. In my heart I believe that Benjamin and I shared a nightmare that was influenced by demonic forces. In the early morning hours of that burdensome day, I held him close with his little head against my chest. Eventually he settled and managed to fall asleep peacefully.

In today's sensationalized culture, I could probably sell a lot of books by talking about how I exorcised the demons right out of that little boy's bedroom. I could tell you tall tales about standing toe-to-toe with the hostile forces around us and chanting the name of Jesus repeatedly like some kind of medieval incantation. Such methods do have a kind of shock-value appeal. But I did none of those things, and I probably never will.

Instead I quietly cried, feeling especially small and helpless in a world so full of evil and powerful, unseen forces. Through my tears I prayed for my little boy. "Father, I can't protect him myself. I'm a weak and frail sinner." In time I just started thinking about Jesus. About His love toward the undeserving. About His grace toward the rebellious. About His agonizing death offered for my horrible sins out of pure love. My mind and heart started to calm. Quietly, I started to sing "Praise the name of Jesus. Praise the name of Jesus. He's my Rock. He's my Fortress. He's my Deliverer. In Him will I trust." There is just something so uplifting about simply focusing on Jesus.

This is how I have decided to teach my children about the upsetting reality of the Devil. He is real. He is powerful. His existence is troubling. But Jesus is so powerful, so supreme, so in control of the entire universe, that we have nothing to fear when we rest in Him. If this book helped you in some small way to increase that simple hope, then I am very grateful. May the name of Jesus be praised!

QUESTIONS FOR REFLECTION

1. The author shared the story of his sermon title "Just Sit Down and Shut Up" and how a well-intended attention-getter backfired. Have you ever had an experience like this?

2. Do you agree that by considering the vile nature of Satan you can better appreciate the beauty and glory of Jesus?

3. Read Matthew 2:1–8. Refer back to the chapter and note the contrast between Jesus, the true king, and Herod, the wannabe king. Does Matthew's "tale of two kings" help you appreciate the character of Jesus more?

4. Read John 10:10. Cite a specific example for the three things the thief does.

5. After reading this book, how has your understanding of Satan been challenged or reshaped? Has your appreciation for Christ's triumph over the Devil been enriched? If so, how?

WHY THE "ARMOR OF GOD" IS NOT A CHAPTER IN THIS BOOK

A book on Satan! Wow, how many chapters are you devoting to the armor of God?"

This was the question a good friend of mine posed over a year ago upon hearing of my preparation for writing this book. To be perfectly honest, I had never really given it much thought before he asked me. And it does seem a bit strange, doesn't it, not to have included the most famous section on spiritual warfare found in the Bible? What was I thinking? Believe it or not, I do have my reasons. And lest you should think that I had checked out mentally, or that I was just plain lazy, I thought it might be helpful to share a bit of my rationale for not including the following passage in my discussion of Satan.

> Finally, be strong in the Lord and in the strength of his might. Put on the whole armor of God, that you may be able to stand against the schemes of the devil. For we do not wrestle against flesh and blood, but against the rulers, against the authorities, against the cosmic powers over this present darkness, against the spiritual forces of evil in the heavenly places. Therefore take up the whole armor of God, that you may be able to withstand in the evil day,

and having done all, to stand firm. Stand therefore, having fastened on the belt of truth, and having put on the breastplate of righteousness, and, as shoes for your feet, having put on the readiness given by the gospel of peace. In all circumstances take up the shield of faith, with which you can extinguish all the flaming darts of the evil one; and take the helmet of salvation, and the sword of the Spirit, which is the word of God, praying at all times in the Spirit, with all prayer and supplication. To that end keep alert with all perseverance, making supplication for all the saints (Ephesians 6:10–18).

The power of God, the armor of God, the schemes of the Devil, the flaming darts of the Evil One, the sword of the Spirit—my friend's question about multiple chapters on this passage makes a lot of sense, doesn't it? So let me give you three reasons why I chose not to include it in this book.

1. I really could not add much to the work of other thinkers and writers.

So many wonderful books, commentaries, and sermons have been written about this famous passage that I found myself thinking, "Come on, Greg, you know you don't have anything else to say." Many of my teaching and preaching heroes have tackled this wonderful text, and I frankly saw little need to throw my far weaker comments in the mix. (For further reading on the subject, see the Recommended Reading list at the end of the book.)

2. The focus of this book is on Christ's victory over Satan, more than on our battling against Satan.

My aim is to put a spotlight on the supremacy and beauty of Jesus Christ. Please understand that I have no objection to books that do focus on the believer's role in spiritual warfare. Yet in my fifteen years as a pastor, I have observed a lopsided interest in our own engagement in the fight. It seems that the majority of resources on the subject of spiritual warfare are intended to satisfy these interests. *Is it time to fight? How should I fight? Is there a way to stop Satan from tearing apart my business, my family, or my church? Can the Devil read my thoughts? How can I specifically pray against them? Should I consider an exorcism?* These questions have their place, but I don't think they are the *best* questions to ask when considering Satan and his role in our lives.

I wanted to explore the wonderful truth of redemption and the implications of Jesus' person and work. *How has the gospel specifically set me free from Satan's domain? How did the life, death, and resurrection of Jesus change the playing field of spiritual warfare? How should I think and feel about the Devil in light of what Jesus has done?* These are the kinds of questions that I wanted to consider in this book.

3. There is a "forest" in Ephesians 6, and I didn't want to get lost in the "trees."

The usual treatment of this passage is to break the armor of God down into its individual components. In a sermon series, for instance, one message would be devoted to the helmet of salvation; another one would be about the breastplate of righteousness, and so forth, the governing thought being that the Christian needs to understand the various pieces of the armor and know how to use them. While I see a compelling argument for this approach, I do not believe that this is the main point of the passage.

There seems to be something buzzing around in Paul's mind when he writes this stirring section. In Isaiah's day, the prophet mourned over the pathetic, shabby condition of Israel's spiritual strength. With vivid words, he surveys the bleak situation.

Justice is turned back,
  and righteousness stands afar off;
for truth has stumbled in the public squares,
  and uprightness cannot enter.
Truth is lacking,
  and he who departs from evil makes himself a prey.
The LORD saw it, and it displeased him that there was no
  justice.
He saw that there was no man,
  and wondered that there was no one to intercede. (Isaiah
  59:14–16a)

Things are bad, to say the least. God sees that there is no justice, righteousness, or truth. Looking for one man to be Israel's
champion, defender, and intercessor, the Lord finds no one—"there
was no one to intercede."

If God's people have no one to fight for them, to turn them
back to righteousness, they are doomed. There is a sense of foreboding disaster in this passage, and the reader should be thinking,
"Oh, no! There must be someone to step in and help." Amazingly,
the next verse tells us that there is.

Then his own arm brought him salvation,
  and his righteousness upheld him. (Isaiah 59:16b)

Just when we thought no one would come to the rescue, God
himself enters the scene and says that "his own arm" will do what
Israel could not do for itself and that "his righteousness" would
stand in for the righteousness the people lacked. The verse is a beautiful picture of the gospel, in which Jesus battles sin and judgment
on our behalf and gives us His own righteousness as a gift. The next
verse in Isaiah's "gospel" is very interesting.

He put on righteousness as a breastplate,
    and a helmet of salvation on His head;
he put on garments of vengeance for clothing,
    and wrapped himself in zeal as a cloak. (Isaiah 59:17)

Seven hundred years before Paul wrote about the armor of God, Isaiah has already told us about a God who dons a breastplate of righteousness and a helmet of salvation. This is the way God dresses for battle when He prepares to fight on behalf of His people.

It is difficult for me to believe that Paul had abandoned this thought when he wrote about the armor of God we need. Rather than analyzing each piece of equipment, I see a greater benefit in highlighting the larger point: God is a warrior and He fights for us. I think this is why Paul stresses that we are to *"be strong in the Lord and in the strength of his might"* (Ephesians 6:10). I see Ephesians 6, then, not so much as a call to battle as a call to trust in God himself when the enemy comes attacking.

The best illustration and application of this idea that I have ever seen comes from Bryan Chapell. I leave you with his inspiring words:

> I can imagine looking out through the faceplate of the helmet of salvation that God has given me. Coming toward me I see the assaulting forces of the Evil One with all his dominions, powers, and authorities. Simply seeing the approaching cloud of darkness from this mighty enemy, I fear that I cannot stand. The ground shakes and my knees begin to buckle. Then, the apostle Paul—like a general on the field of battle—calls out, "Steady now. Do not retreat. Take your stand. Be strong, in the power of his might. Forget the strength you thought you could provide. Remember the might of the armor God has given you. Resurrection

power has given you a breastplate of his righteousness, the shield of faith, feet that are shod with readiness that comes from being at peace with the Sovereign of the universe. Beyond all of these defenses, he has given you an ultimate weapon, the sword of the Spirit that is the Word of God. Now, confident of the strength and integrity of the armor that you have been given, stand firm."[1]

1. Bryan Chapell, *Holiness by Grace* (Wheaton, IL: Crossway, 2001), 147.

RECOMMENDED READING

Joel Beeke, *Striving Against Satan* (Evangelical Press, 2006).
This is perhaps the most accessible, concise, biblically sound book on the subject of Satan today. Beeke is a terrific writer and presents almost a mini systematic theology on the Devil and spiritual warfare. Well-researched, with excellent applications and illustrations, this is an important book for building a strong understanding of Satan and his role in the world.

Thomas Brooks, *Precious Remedies Against Satan's Devices* (Banner of Truth, 2000). Though hundreds of years old, Brooks' treatment of Satan's methods and the believers "remedies" is still the most thorough and helpful resource on the subject. Initially, I considered making *Living Free in Enemy Territory* a modern paraphrase of Brooks' classic. Honestly, it was too high a mountain. This classic stands on its own.

Frederick Leahy, *Satan Cast Out* (Banner of Truth, 1990).
Perhaps the number-one best kept secret on the list. A short book, Leahy's best contribution to the discussion of the spiritual realm is by pointing out many of the extreme and mystical approaches many writers adopt when discussing spiritual warfare. While Leahy goes a little further in his critique than I would, his rationale is compelling and worthy of a careful read.

C. S. Lewis, *The Screwtape Letters* (HarperCollins, 1996).

A must-have classic. Lewis brilliantly illustrates the goals, tactics, and subtleties of spiritual warfare from the mouth of Screwtape, a senior-level demon mentoring his nephew Wormwood in the art of temptation and sabotage. In a provocative manner, some of the most moving prose about God's goodness and character come by way of Screwtape describing his "Enemy."

Ray Stedman, *Spiritual Warfare* (Discovery House, 1999).

In his clear and thoughtful prose, Stedman does what some may have been wanting to see in the book you are holding. Largely an exposition of the "armor of God" passage in Ephesians, Stedman's book is very good in helping the reader think through the implications of each piece of the armor. He is wonderfully faithful to Scripture and a great storyteller.

ABOUT THE AUTHOR

Greg serves as the senior pastor of Christ Fellowship Church in Fallston, Maryland, a church he planted in 2003. His passion is to teach the Word of God in a deep yet culturally engaging way. Greg has been deeply influenced by pastors John Piper, Tim Keller, Mark Driscoll, and John MacArthur. His greatest concern for the future of the church is that it not lose its grip on the centrality of the gospel, the glory of God, and the necessity of expository Bible teaching.

Greg is thankful for the "gift" of insomnia that allows him to write books in the wee hours of the morning. His wife, Lisa, is also thankful for those writing hours so she doesn't have to hear him snore. Greg and Lisa are blessed with four children: Samantha, Benjamin, Isaac, and Ella Grace. It's hard to get a word in edgewise at the Dutcher house, but it just wouldn't feel like home without the chaos.

What readers are saying about *You Are the Treasure That I Seek: But There's a Lot of Cool Stuff Out There, Lord* by Greg Dutcher:

"This book first frightens, then entrances, then liberates. It frightens as it lays bare the hidden idols of the heart. It entrances with the promise of a treasure worth more than all our idols put together. And ultimately, it liberates with a vision of Christ so compelling and so powerful that the reader says, 'O Lord, set me free and I will be free indeed.' It's easy to make people feel guilty about their idols. Greg Dutcher inspires us to set aside our trinkets in pursuit of the Ultimate Treasure."

—Dr. Ray Pritchard, president of Keep Believing Ministries and author of *An Anchor for the Soul*, *The Healing Power of Forgiveness*, and *He's God and We're Not*

"The first two commandments and the cautionary history of ancient Israel should set our hearts at their highest level of alert against idolatry. Perhaps we are more sophisticated than our forefathers who made wood and stone images of their gods—but ours are no less deadly for being invisible. We need to drag them out into the light and smash them to pieces in repentance. Greg Dutcher's book serves as a set of 'night-vision goggles' to help us root these insidious idols out of our hearts. Then he goes further and restores and renews us in full-fledged adoration of Jesus."

—Kris Lundgaard, author of *The Enemy Within*

"Of the making of books that make us feel better there is no end, but books that actually make us better are rare. Greg Dutcher has done the rare thing: journeyed into the heart of darkness—our penchant for idols—and then blazed a trail back into daylight. He dares to tell us the bad news about ourselves in order that we can hear, clear and fresh, the good news in spite of ourselves."

—Mark Buchanan, author of *The Rest of God: Restoring Your Soul by Restoring Sabbath* and *Hidden in Plain Sight*

"Greg Dutcher's book is excellent. It is biblical in content and very well written. It is wonderful that Greg has made the subject so accessible. He is a master of illustration. The discussion of the idols of our lives leads to a strong affirmation of the gospel. This book would be great for adult or high school Bible studies or as a gift for an inquirer."

—Dr. John Frame, professor of systematic theology and philosophy, Reformed Theological Seminary, and author of *The Doctrine of God* and *Salvation Belongs to the Lord*

"This is a great book (and a needed one), and Greg's writing is crisp and fun."

—Dr. Steve Brown, nationally syndicated talk-show host, Key Life Network

NOTE TO THE READER

The publisher invites you to share your response to the message of this book by writing Discovery House Publishers, P.O. Box 3566, Grand Rapids, MI 49501, USA. For information about other Discovery House books, music, videos, or DVDs, contact us at the same address or call 1-800-653-8333. Find us on the Internet at http://www.dhp.org/ or send e-mail to books@dhp.org.